Fifty Years

of

Silence No More

*A Journal by Bob Jacobs, a Middle-Aged Medium,
Describing His Unbelievably True Life Story, and
His Journey with God, Heaven, and Spirit.*

BOB JACOBS

BALBOA.
PRESS

A DIVISION OF HAY HOUSE

Balboa Press books may be ordered through booksellers or by contacting:

Balboa Press
A Division of Hay House
1663 Liberty Drive
Bloomington, IN 47403
www.balboapress.com
1 (877) 407-4847

Because of the dynamic nature of the Internet, any web addresses or
links contained in this book may have changed since publication and
may no longer be valid. The views expressed in this work are solely those
of the author and do not necessarily reflect the views of the publisher,
and the publisher hereby disclaims any responsibility for them.

The author of this book does not dispense medical advice or prescribe the use
of any technique as a form of treatment for physical, emotional, or medical
problems without the advice of a physician, either directly or indirectly. The
intent of the author is only to offer information of a general nature to help
you in your quest for emotional and spiritual well-being. In the event you use
any of the information in this book for yourself, which is your constitutional
right, the author and the publisher assume no responsibility for your actions.

Any people depicted in stock imagery provided by Getty Images are
models, and such images are being used for illustrative purposes only.
Certain stock imagery © Getty Images.

Print information available on the last page.

ISBN: 978-1-5043-9928-9 (sc)
ISBN: 978-1-5043-9930-2 (hc)
ISBN: 978-1-5043-9929-6 (e)

Library of Congress Control Number: 2018902748

Balboa Press rev. date: 03/05/2018

Contents

Contents

The artwork on the front cover of this book
is the work of Jennifer Jacobs.

A big thank you to Jennifer Jacobs and Sharon Gullett
for their help with the editing of this book.

Dedication

I dedicate this journal to my first wife, Cathy, and my son, David, who were taken from this life on earth at a very young age.

I dedicate this journal to my father. If it weren't for his love, caring, and being there for me as a young boy, I don't think that I could have made it through the challenges of my life.

I dedicate this journal to my mother, who I watched struggle to take care of my father in those later years.

I dedicate this journal to Wilma and her four daughters, Kathy, Teresa, Kelly, and Pam. If it weren't for them I would have never told my story. I can't thank you enough.

I dedicate this journal to Joshua. As you will see in this journal, Joshua touched my heart, as did his mother, Lisa, and his father, Marty.

I dedicate this journal to my wife, Barbara, my daughters, Hollee and Jennifer, my son-in-law, Justin, my granddaughter, Madison, and the rest of my extended family. The truth of my life is written in these pages.

Bob Jacobs

Foreword

Have you ever wondered if the afterlife is real? Could Spirit Guides and Guardian Angels be real? Is there a God and Heaven? Can anybody develop or have the Sixth Sense? Are some people born with a special gift? Do children have a sense of knowing? I will let you be the judge of these questions and let you answer them for yourself after reading my fascinating journal.

Introduction

This book will take you on a journey. The journey will be about events that have happened in my life and I will take you from my early years as a child to the present day. In most cases, I will use actual names. Some names have been changed in order to protect people's identities. I will not alter or exaggerate any story or fact; all stories and details in this book are fact. I am not a writer, I am a factory worker. These events started when I was five years old, and possibly even earlier than that. As you will see in the story, I had a lot of tragedy in my life between the ages of 18 and 23. Don't get me wrong, I'm not complaining, I just want you to understand why I shut this gift down for so long. All I wanted was to be normal and have a normal life. I kept every event in my life a secret until I was 50 years old. Not a single person on this planet knew my story, not even my wife of over 25 years. I figured that I would take my story with me to my grave, that is, until after the event with Wilma. Wilma changed my life and so I had to tell my story. It is so unbelievable. This is why I keep stating that everything is fact. It is so incredible that even I would have a hard time believing it, if I didn't know it to be true.

CHAPTER ONE

The Beginning

I was born in the Midwest, in 1964. My parents were raised in the country (rural areas) with not having much more than a roof over their heads and food in their bellies. Now don't get me wrong, you shouldn't judge a person's intellect by where they came from or what they had. Both of my parents had a high school diploma or its equivalency. They were fortunate enough to get good factory jobs when I was growing up. The sixties and seventies provided a lot of factory jobs in our area during that era that didn't require a college education and paid a decent wage. I have two siblings. We grew up in a small three bedroom, one bath, brick ranch house, with our parents in a newer subdivision. We were lucky. Our house's backyard bordered a small horse farm. On the other side of the horse farm was a public park, probably close to 200 acres. The park had a lake, basketball and tennis courts, woods with trails, and playgrounds. It was a great place to grow up. Back in those days, school was released for the summer around Memorial Day and didn't resume until after Labor Day. Between those two holidays, about the only time that I was inside the house was to sleep. I loved to be outside.

Presently, I am married to my wife, Barbara. We have been married for over 28 years. She is a beautiful, dark haired woman. I am an assembly line worker in a factory and she is a teacher's aide. We have two daughters, Hollee and Jennifer. Hollee is married to

Justin, and they have our only grandchild, Madison. Madison is now five years old. Jennifer is still at home with us, starting her last year of college. We also have a Miniature Australian Shepherd, Lexi.

When I was five years old, I was horse playing with my dad. I just happened to ask him why I couldn't see out of my right eye. Come to find out, after some doctor's appointments, I had a tumor behind that eye. Well, of course, the tumor had to be removed and in doing so, they had to completely remove my right eye. I was fitted with a prosthetic eye and life went on. The only thing that I remember about the operation was the bright operating room light. At least, that is what I thought it was. We will re-visit this in more detail much later in the book. If the tumor hadn't been caught, it could have grown and caused complete blindness or other problems. Was this just luck? Or maybe a guardian angel watching over me? Some people might say, "What do you mean luck, you lost an eye!" Well, I have always felt fortunate just to have one eye. Don't ask me why, I just have.

The year was 1972, and my hand was cusped over my right eye. I was eight years old, at elementary school, and my prosthetic eye had fallen out. I didn't know how to put it back in, and in a state of panic, I went up and explained the situation to my teacher. I have never forgotten the compassion that this teacher showed me. She was a young, beautiful, talented teacher that everybody loved. She directed me to wait out in the hallway while she got help. I waited out in the hallway until my teacher came back with the principal of the school. My dad was the only one who knew how to position my eye back into place and I knew that he was at work. It was only about 30 minutes until school was to be dismissed. My siblings and I had always rode the bus, carpooled with other kids' moms, or rode with our mom to and from school. Next, the principal walked me out to where my mother would usually pick us up in the parking lot. Instead of mom being in the car waiting to pick us up, there sat our dad. This was odd because he **never** picked us up from school; I couldn't believe it. He immediately positioned my eye back into place. I jumped in the car and waited on my siblings. End of story, it was over. I had never felt so relieved. Now stop right here and think for a moment. My dad *never* picked us up from school. This was the only time that he picked us up, and the only time this ever happened. Yet my dad, who never picked us up, was there. He was the *only one* who could have fixed the situation. That was the first time I felt like there was a presence watching over me. Was God or a guardian angel watching over me?

Other than having one eye, I had a normal childhood. I played basketball and baseball, ran track, fished, hunted, got involved in long distance running, and had other interests. I was a healthy and happy kid. My parents stayed together and made a nice home life for us three kids including camping trips and a few other vacations. We were just a regular middle class family and I was never treated differently by my parents because of my eye. This, I was thankful for, because I just wanted to be a normal kid.

In the summer of 1976, I was playing baseball. My dad was the coach and my mom was in the bleachers. This was normal because I played every year. My dad coached me in other sports as well. I didn't realize it at the time, but he was probably trying to stay close to me just in case something happened with my eye, though it never did. One day, I was in the batter's box facing the hardest throwing pitcher in the league. In the background noise from the bleachers, I heard someone say, "He's cross eyed." I think they were sitting on the front row between home plate and first base. At the same time, the pitch was released, I swung my bat and hit the ball. It was a pop fly into left center field, very high in the air. As I headed for first base, I heard (in my mind) the Voice tell me, "This is for you." At that exact instance, a gust of wind took the fly ball way past the outfield fence for a homerun. I know that sounds strange, but that is exactly what happened. That was the only homerun in my baseball career. That was the only time that I ever heard a nasty remark about my eye from the crowd. More importantly, that was the first time I heard "The Voice." It was a kind of nonverbal voice that I understood, but was

3

sent to me telepathically. I never told a soul. Now pause for a second and consider, is this a coincidence? I don't think so. Well, enough said about my eye, this story isn't about my lack of vision. Actually, it is about me having vision, but of a different nature.

When I was about 14 years old, I was on the middle school basketball team. It was a cold winter day and after school I went to basketball practice. When I got home, I went downstairs where my dad was watching the news. I had homework to do. I needed to read a book for the next day. I was tired, so I told my dad that I was going to take a short nap on the couch and then read my book. In doing so, I placed the book under my head and quickly dozed off. When I woke up, I opened the book, which I had **never read**, and began to read through it. *I knew everything in the book!* It was as if I had already read it at least once. I explained to my dad what had just happened about the book being under my head and how I must have read it while I was sleeping. He just kind of laughed it off and told me that I should start doing my homework like that every day. He didn't take me seriously. Now that I look back, I can't say that I blame him. I mean, who would believe that? I knew how significant and serious it was. It was real. I knew right there and then that I had some kind of special gift. I didn't understand it, but I knew it was there from that day forward.

Throughout those early years of my life there were other things that happened to me, but I will just mention one more so that we can move forward with the story. At a young age, I remember telling my dad that if I put one finger from each hand really close together until they were almost touching, I could see white stuff floating between them. I also told him that I could see an outline around everything that I looked at. He kind of played me off and changed the subject. I think he didn't understand and didn't know what to say. Now, after thinking about it, he probably thought that it had something to do with me having one eyed vision. I now understand what I was seeing as a child. I was seeing the energy fields around everything. I was probably also starting to see auras.

Auras are colors that are seen by some individuals in the energy field of objects or people. Not understanding this at the time and having no one to explain it to me, I kept my mouth shut and just tried to turn it off. I knew that I was different. I already was different. I just wanted to be normal. I kind of ignored my gift and probably tuned it out for the next several years. I never told anybody about any of those experiences. Life went on and I grew up on through my teenage years.

CHAPTER TWO

Hard Times

Growing up through middle school, I basically kept straight A's, never missed a day, and stayed out of trouble. Everything was too easy for me. So, about my freshman year I started getting into trouble. I decided that I wanted to see how the rougher cut kids lived and I turned to a different path. By the time I was a junior in high school, I was a hardcore hippie. Hey, it was 1981, and my last chance to experience the hippie era. I smoked pot, drank, and experimented with a few other drugs. I was just out having fun. I never got hooked on anything, except cigarettes, but had a good time. Someone, later in life, told me that I was good in sports and asked me why I turned for a few years. I told him that I was good in sports and I also was good at being a hippie. I told him that I was an "All American" in *hippie*.

At the age of 18, I fell in love with my high school sweetheart, Cathy. She was a blonde haired beauty. Cathy came from a big family; they were good people. I have never to this day been around another family that stuck together like they did. Hats off to them, that is very rare. Just a few months out of high school, I got Cathy pregnant. We got married soon after, and six months later, our son, David Ray, was born. I got a job as a stock person at a grocery store. It didn't pay much, but it had medical insurance and that is what I needed. I had always worked, probably since I was 14, but I needed a job with insurance. Eventually, I was named stock crew manager. This position still didn't pay well, but we had a mobile home and a dependable vehicle. I spent time with my son. I took him fishing, camping, miniature golfing, and read him stories at bedtime. I eventually got moved up to shift manager at the grocery store and we had enough money to pay our bills, but that was about it.

When I was about 20 years old, my dad took sick with a very high fever of 107 degrees. He went into a coma for a few months and was in the hospital for about five months. The high fever fried his brain. It was a form of encephalitis that went up through his spinal cord and attacked his brain. As a result, he was paralyzed from the waist down and his brain functioned like that of a small toddler. He was taken care of like this for 15 years by my mom, my siblings, myself, and our spouses. That is the point in my life when I really grew up. I had no one to lean on. Dad was down and mom was busy taking care of him. I knew right then at the age of 19 or 20 that I was officially on my own. I still to this day feel empathetic for any young person who has lost a parent, is an orphan, or has obstacles put in their path of life. It really does make life harder. After 15 years of living like this, my dad did pass to the other side and I must say that I was relieved that the whole ordeal was over. We loved our dad, and still do, but what a terrible situation. I can remember taking care of dad so that mom could go do things outside of the house. I will always remember thinking that my peers, we were in our early twenties, were out having fun, and I was at my mom's house tying my dad's hands to his hospital bed so that I could change his diaper without him rubbing his hands in the mess.

During these same few years when I was between the ages of 18 and 23, I had an uncle get stabbed in the chest, another uncle have his leg blown off, and another relative get shot in the head. None of these incidents had anything to do with what I will call "my gift", but I am mentioning them so that you understand that I had a lot going on in my life. I turned my gift off and dealt with life.

When I was 22 years old, I was working in the grocery store

one evening and I got a call from the hospital. They told me that I needed to get there right away. Upon arriving, I was told by a law enforcement officer that my wife, Cathy, had been killed in an automobile accident. I asked the officer, "What, did she just run off in a ditch or something?" He then stated that she was hit head on by a drunk driver. I turned around in disbelief and hit the wall with the bottom of my fist. Immediately, I thought about David. They were always together. I asked the officer, "What about my boy, where is he, is he alright?" He said that he was flown to another hospital where he was in intensive care. By this time my mom had arrived at the hospital. I told her we needed to get to the other hospital where David was. For some reason, I was paralyzed but mom got us a ride to the hospital from some family friends. I now call them angels. When we arrived at the second hospital, David was barely hanging on. He was being kept alive by a life support system. During this time, I still remember sitting in this tiny chapel at the hospital with Cathy's dad. We were in there together by ourselves. I don't think either one of us said a word. We just looked at each other in disbelief. I can still remember to this day that at that time, I was thinking, "I'm losing it, I'm losing it."

Twenty four hours later, I was told that David would not recover. They said if I kept him on life support to keep him alive, he would be in a vegetative state, and be paralyzed from the neck down for the rest of his life. After seeing that decision being made with my dad, I decided right away to let him go. They unplugged the machines and I held him in my arms. I rocked him on a wooden rocking chair. He still had tubes, medicine, and bandages on him. As long as I live I will never forget the smell of that medicine. It is something that just never went away. I told him to tell Mommy that I loved her. I told him that I loved him. I rocked him in that chair as he took his last breaths, wrapped in a little blanket that the wonderful nurses put on him. I kissed him on the forehead and he was gone. I handed him to one of the nurses and walked out of the room into the hallway. I will always remember when I walked into the hallway that my uncle was there. He looked at me with hope, but quickly realized by looking at me that David was gone. I walked down the hospital hallway alone. I needed to be alone. In twenty four hours, I had lost my 22 year old wife and 3 ½ year old son. ***Nothing, and I mean nothing else in the world mattered***. Cathy was a great wife and mother. She always put David first. She truly cared about people. To this day, I have not regretted making that decision. I made the right decision.

About two weeks before the accident, Cathy had a premonition. She basically told me what was going to happen. She had this premonition in a dream. Keep this in mind for later in the story. She definitely was intuitive.

Life had dealt me a lot of blows at an early age. I was just under 23 years old. Anyway, that was life and I dealt with it and went on. It wasn't easy, but what else could I do, give up?

This is a picture of Cathy, David, and myself.

CHAPTER THREE

The Funeral

Now this is where my gift took it up another notch. After all these years I never told a soul about this next event until I wrote this book. At Cathy and David's funeral, the choir was singing a song in the church. It was a pretty crowded service. A lot of the community showed up to pay their respects to my wife and son. As the choir sang, I could hear "Barbara" singing the song along with them, but it was as though she was singing *louder* than the rest of them. It was like the rest of the voices were kind of muffled out. I saw "Barb" in my mind's eye. This is when the Voice told me word for word, ***"This is who you are going to marry next."*** I couldn't actually see Barb, she was off to the side, and out of my line of vision. I looked around totally in shock to see if anybody else heard what I had just heard. What I heard was clear and simply undeniable. Obviously, they didn't hear what I heard so I shrugged it off and continued my grieving process. I thought maybe I was losing my mind. I didn't think about what had happened at all after that. I had enough to deal with already. I think I blocked it out of my mind. I worked in the same grocery store as Barb, but I didn't know her at all. It wasn't as if I was hitting on her or anything at work. I was married, had a son, and was just trying to pay the bills.

A month or so later, I found David's toy jacks and ball on the bathroom floor in our trailer. He had just gotten these right before the accident. They were in the middle of the floor like they had just been played with recently. Now I know that I was in shock during this time period, but I had been in that bathroom every day. If you step on a set of jacks, you know it, period. So yes, I do believe that David's spirit was there physically moving his toys. My grieving and loneliness period that I went through were not easy. It was down right rough. But, as I mentioned earlier, what could I do? You go on with your life and deal with it.

About eight months later, somebody at the store where I worked told me to ask Barb out for a date. This person's name was Lisa. Keep Lisa's name in mind because later in the book there is a huge story I have to tell about her. I took Lisa's advice and asked Barb out. I never even thought about the Voice talking to me at the funeral. It never even crossed my mind. Well, guess what? It is now 29 years later and I have been married to Barb for 28 years. Barb is a beautiful dark haired woman. I have been blessed with two wonderful women in my life. Barb is top notch. She would do anything for anybody. And, like Cathy, she always put our children first.

Now this story gets even more bizarre. This is another story that I have never told a soul, at least not until I wrote this book. Right about the same time that Barb and I got married, we were asleep in our bed. I was awakened out of my sleep and there was a bluish white light in our room. I sat up in bed, and Cathy appeared in the light. Her spirit had manifested right in front of me. I couldn't believe what I was seeing. It was the first time in my life that I couldn't believe what I was seeing. I rubbed my eye in disbelief. She was there in the bedroom with us, right at the foot of the bed. She was clothed in what looked like a flowing light blue gown that was wavering in the light. I didn't see her feet. It was like she was floating through the air in the blue light from about the waist up. She was moving from left to right. At that time, she communicated with me, telepathically. She saw Barb in the bed with me and told me, "***It was okay and that she understood***." She wanted me to go on with my life. I had gone on with my life, but somehow she knew that I was carrying that guilt of remarrying around with me. She communicated a feeling of peace to me; and she and the light disappeared into the bedroom wall. Like I said, this was the first time in my life that I couldn't believe what I saw. You might find this funny, but I thought about "Gilligan's Island" after it happened because Gilligan was always rubbing his eyes when he saw something odd. I always thought how fake this looked when he did this. But I found out that this is what a person does when they don't believe what they see. It really shook me, but I kept my mouth shut and never told a soul. Barb slept through the entire event and I never mentioned it to her. This gift I had was getting stronger. I didn't know what to do, so not wanting to be ridiculed I kept everything to myself. I figured that I had had enough stuff happen to me in my life and I didn't need anything else to complicate it further. I tried to just turn this gift off and live my life and be normal for a change.

For the next 25 years I did just that. Barb and I had two daughters to raise, and a life of our own. I figured that I should put all of my energy into raising my new family. I learned from the first time around that you can't go back. We raised our girls in an older, stone house. It had a pool, a pond, and a big yard. There was plenty of fresh air to go around. Hollee and Jennifer were on the high school dance team so we spent our time going to ballgames. It was a perfect fit. Barb and I were both athletes, as teenagers, so going to ballgames was right up our alley. We had a lot of fun throughout those years. I was focused on my family, not my gift.

Now there were many times over those 25 years where things did happen, and I will list just a few. I tried to just ignore my gift. There was the time that I dreamed about a light, like a flashlight, shining on a deer. That was the night that my 3D deer target was stolen out of our yard. *There were times that I repeated things back to people that they had never told me, only to have them tell me I was right, but that they never had told me those things.* I have on several occasions sensed that someone was calling on the phone, told Barb, and five minutes later, they called. My dad and grandma have appeared to me. They have also contacted me in dreams. There was just this feeling of intuition that would never go away. It was a sense of *knowing*. I have always been drawn to the paranormal my entire life. I had always, throughout my life, looked up at the stars, and thought there is so much more out there to learn in this universe. This story gets even more peculiar in the next chapter. Even after being watched over, communicated to, having spirits manifest right in front of me, and having this odd gift, the real story is just now starting.

CHAPTER FOUR

Heaven, the Light, the Energy, and the Love

As I have mentioned, I have always had a fascination with the paranormal. Over the years I have read several books about the subject including a few about Edgar Cayce. He was a modern prophet that was able to connect to the *Akashic Records*. The Akashic Records are supposedly a conscious record of every event that has ever happened on Earth. It's like a database of information, except it is stored in a higher consciousness instead of a computer bank. I also read several other books, including the Bible. If you ever want to become more spiritual, I do suggest reading the Bible. By the time you finish, it will change your life. I have always wondered what heaven was like, as I'm sure a lot of people have. On the night of October 27, 2014, I had an experience that was life changing.

Since I get up at 4:30 am to get ready for work, I usually try to lay down in bed by 9:00 pm or so. On the night of October 27, 2014, I did just that. I laid down a little early that night, and this is exactly what happened while I was sleeping. First, I will set the stage a little so that you can understand the story easier. My sister-in-law, whom we will call Teresa, (because her name is Teresa), lost her mother, Wilma, about 15 months earlier. At the funeral home when Barb and I visited Wilma, I spoke to her telepathically and told her, "You are a good person and we love you." I didn't know if I had gotten through to her or not. I never thought much more about it after that.

While asleep that night on October 27, I found myself in an unfamiliar place. I looked up from the ground and saw Wilma. I said, "Well hello Wilma, what are you doing here?" At the same time, I realized something very odd was going on, and it seemed like time stood still. It seemed as if I were in a different time and space. I gained so much information in what seemed like the blink of an eye.

As I looked at Wilma, she sent me messages without speaking. She spoke to me telepathically. She wanted her four daughters to know that she was alright. She had a small child on her lap. The child winked at me with its left eye. As it did so, a flash of light came out of its eye. At this point, I didn't know if the child was a girl or boy. This young child though, will come up in a later chapter. Everything around me was in very vivid colors. Next, I saw Wilma by herself, laying back on a very green grassed hillside. It was beautiful. She had on a pretty red shirt and blue jean shorts. Wilma was at peace. This was the message that she was wanting passed onto her girls. As I was with Wilma, the colors were so pronounced, it was amazing. But what really blew me away was **the light that I was in**; it was a bright light. This light was not blinding, but a bright light that affected everything around you. It wasn't like the Sun; it was a light that surrounded you. **It went through my soul**. It was like I was taking a bath or swimming in this light. That is exactly how it felt. It was amazing. At the same time as I was feeling (Notice that I said *feeling*. I didn't just see this light, I *felt* it.) this wonderful light, **there was a positive energy buzz going through my entire body**. I felt this positive energy down to my core. It really seemed to be pronounced in my mind. It was so incredible, I don't even know how to describe it so that you can understand. All I could feel and think about while all of this was going on was love, joy, happiness, and peace. I just can't say enough about how I felt during this experience. I was feeling this, **"Warming, loving, kind, gentle light"**, going through my entire body and soul. At the same time, I had this unbelievable positive energy flow going through my entire body, soul, and mind. The only way that I can describe what I felt is with these words, *"Unbelievable, Love, Joy, Peace, Happiness, and Positive Energy."* That doesn't even do it justice. Take those words times one thousand and it still doesn't make you understand what I felt. This light and energy had a presence I felt. Not just saw, but felt!

As all of this was going on, I was in a narrow, colorful area. I noticed that on the fringe area of this vivid color and wonderful place that I was in, was an unclear area. It was kind of foggy or misty and sort of fuzzy and grey. I felt the presence of someone in this fuzzy area. It was a male. I couldn't see him, but I could feel his presence. At first, I couldn't figure out who it was. *Then he, or this presence, let me know that it was Albert.* Albert was Wilma's husband and Teresa's dad. At first, I thought it was AJ. AJ, or Albert Jacob, was named after Albert. AJ is Teresa's son. I thought, "What is AJ doing here?" Then it hit me. It wasn't AJ, it was Albert. All I could do was feel Albert's presence. I couldn't see him. He was letting me know that he was with Wilma. He let me know that he was by her side and he wasn't going anywhere. He wanted to make sure that I knew that. At the same time that I was communicating with Albert, I noticed at the top of the hill, also in the fuzzy fringe area, was a group of people standing. They were letting me know that they were Wilma's relatives. They wanted Teresa and her sisters to know that their mom was not alone. She was with her husband, Albert, and other relatives. It was as if Albert brought Wilma down from the hillside to communicate with me. I did notice that one of the male relatives was tall and thin. I also noticed that there were one or two children in the group. These items will also come up in a later chapter.

About the time all of this was starting to sink into my mind, and I was starting to understand what was going on, *it hit me. I was in the afterlife and heaven!* I thought, *"What am I doing here? Did I just die?"* Well, don't ask me why, but that thought put me into a tailspin. The next thing I know I was lying in bed gasping for air; I couldn't breathe. I have awakened from dreams gasping for air before, but not like this. After catching my breath, realizing where I was, and regaining my senses, I jumped out of bed. In a state of panic and confusion, I went out to the living room where Barb, my daughter, Jennifer, and my granddaughter, Madison, were watching television. I wanted to make sure everybody was okay and things were real and normal. After a reality check, I looked at the clock and it was only 10:00 pm. I had just dozed off for a short while and all of this happened during this short slumber.

Let me make it real clear here. ***This event changed my life!*** I will never be the same again. I have been through a lot in my life. I have lost loved ones, felt presence my whole life, seen spirit manifestations right in front of me, and have been spoken to telepathically throughout my life. Yet, this was different. This was way different! ***I had been to the afterlife and back!*** Let me repeat that; ***I had been to the afterlife and back!*** I now not only knew that the afterlife was ***real***, but I knew what it **felt** like. Again, let me repeat that; ***I knew what it felt like.*** During this experience, I didn't see God, but I felt his presence. I don't think God is a person. He is a presence. But, just because I didn't see God as a person, doesn't mean that he isn't. I am just explaining my experience exactly as it happened. ***Here is my take on it, "God is the LIGHT. God is the EVERLASTING LIGHT. God is the EVERYTHING." "God is LOVE." That is the best way that I can describe it. "God is the EVERYTHING!" While I was standing in the white light, I knew that I was standing with God. I didn't have to be told this. I just knew it!*** Even after all of this, I kept my mouth shut, just like I had my entire life, and didn't tell anybody about what happened.

CHAPTER FIVE

The Letter

This event affected me like no other in my life. I went on to work and tried to function normally. This time, for the first time in my life, I couldn't. I am a 6 foot, 240 pound big guy. I was at work on the assembly line and literally crying while I was doing my job. I had on my safety glasses and kept my head down, making sure nobody noticed. But every time that I thought about what had happened, I would start crying. This was the first time in my life that I was given a message that wasn't for me. It was eating away at me. I was feeling guilty for not passing on this message to Teresa and her three sisters. Finally, after about a week, I decided to break the "Fifty Years of Silence." I typed a letter to Teresa explaining my experience with her mom, Wilma. I then took it out to the living room where I let Barb read it. This was very difficult for me to break my silence of 50 years. No one on the planet knew about this part of my life except me. Not even Barb, my wife of over 25 years. I knew that it would be a life changing step for me, but I also knew that I had to do it. While Barb was reading the letter, she began to cry. She knew that I was serious and not playing around. I had her text Teresa and tell her that I had a letter for her if she could come pick it up. This was out of the ordinary for me and Teresa knew it.

When Teresa pulled into our driveway, I was outside waiting for her. She rolled her window down in the car and looked at me with a lot of fear and anxiety. She had no idea what this was about. I told her that I couldn't look at her, because that this was too emotional for me. Of course, this only heightened her anxiety and fear. I told her that this letter would change her and her three sisters' lives forever. I told her not to tell anybody about the letter and that she was never even at my house. I didn't put my name on the letter. I was afraid if someone else saw it they would be able to identify me. This was a big step for me. I thought, as usual, everybody would think that I was losing my mind, even her. I didn't care, I had to do this. I felt relieved. I did what Wilma wanted me to do. It felt good knowing that I had passed on a loving message to help people. I didn't care if they believed it or not. My job was done, or so I thought.

Teresa later texted us. She said that she believed in this kind of stuff and she would share the letter with her sisters. ***Teresa later told me that when her mom was dying, she told them that if there was a way for her to make contact with Teresa and her sisters, she would do it.*** They loved their mom. She was all they had. They lost their dad, Albert, to a heart attack, when he was in his forties, and they were all still young. When Wilma passed, they lost their world, or so they thought. I'm sure there was a lot of skepticism when they first read that letter. What happened next would erase that skepticism in their minds forever.

Was this heaven? Yes, it absolutely was. ***For some reason God let me feel what it was like in his light. Why me? I don't know.*** I think maybe God knew it would take this kind of experience to awaken my soul and spirit. Whatever the case, I feel very fortunate to have felt the presence of God and heaven. Now this is where the story really takes off.

About a month after I gave Teresa the letter, I was still feeling caught up in the whole event. I was constantly feeling the presence of Wilma. It would not go away. Even when driving home from work I could feel her presence in my car a few times. It was like she wasn't going to leave me alone until I told her daughters more. It wasn't a bad presence, but it was there. I decided to type Teresa and her sisters another letter. A bunch of us (our families) were meeting at a restaurant for dinner to celebrate a niece graduating from college. At the time, nobody else in the family knew about the event so I secretly put the letter in Teresa's purse. I told her so that she knew about it. To tell you the truth, I kind of felt like some kind of secret agent or something.

Here is what the letter contained. I went into more detail about the night of the event with Wilma. I wanted to make sure that I told Teresa and her sisters everything. I was afraid if something happened to me the whole truth would be lost forever. I wanted them to know everything. I told them that Wilma wasn't going to leave me alone until I told them more. She wanted to leave no doubt in their minds that she was reaching out to connect to them. I told them that it reminded me of the movie "Ghost" with Patrick Swayze where he wouldn't leave Ida Mae alone until she did what he wanted. I also told them that a phrase had been going through my mind ever since that October night that wouldn't go away. I told them that Wilma was telling me this phrase was meant for all four of the daughters. The phrase was, "Remember, Taylor, every time a bell rings, an angel gets its wings." Taylor is Teresa's niece. Teresa's sisters' names are Kathy, Kelly, and Pam. Taylor is Pam's preteen daughter and Wilma's granddaughter. I thought maybe the phrase had something to do with the movie "It's a Wonderful Life." I thought maybe Wilma and Taylor had watched the movie together or something. Here was Teresa, Kathy, Kelly, and Pam's (from now on I may refer to these sisters as *Wilma's girls*) response. They said they were a little skeptical of my first letter. I can't say that I blame them because I really didn't know Wilma all that well. We invited, and she came, to all of our big parties and we loved her. We really weren't around her that much, but I always felt a connection between us.

Wilma's girls said that "Ghost" was Wilma's favorite movie. It came out right after their dad, Albert, passed away to the other side. They also said that when their mom, Wilma, was alive, every time they all went to visit relatives at the cemetery, ***Wilma would ring*** *a bell and say, "Every time a bell rings, an angel gets its wings."* Now that just blew me away! What are the odds? And that isn't all. *They also told me that Taylor keeps a bell right above her bed and rings it for her grandmother, Wilma, all the time.* Are you kidding me? Let me say it again. Are you kidding me? This is information that there is no way I could have known. *I think at this point we all knew that Wilma had fulfilled her death bed promise of finding a way to connect with her daughters after she passed to the other side. I told the girls in the letters that I had had previous experiences in my life before Wilma's. I told them that she must have known that after passing and found a way to connect to me.* This is just the beginning of the journey. There is so much more in the coming chapters that is just unbelievable. But before that, I will spend some time explaining what I did next so that it sets the stage for the rest of the book.

Top: This is a picture of Wilma.

Bottom: This is a picture of Wilma and her husband Ick (Albert).

CHAPTER SIX

Learning to Connect

After the second letter, I decided that I would try to get back to this wonderful place of the afterlife with Wilma. I had meditated on and off throughout my entire life. Don't ask me why, I just had. Some of the meditation I had done was when I was involved in martial arts. Most of it was something I just picked up on my own out of my own interest. Remember, I was always fascinated with the paranormal. So I started trying to connect with Wilma again. I did this for a couple of months. I never did get back to what I will call heaven, but I did make it back. And boy, did I make it back.

At the same time, during this two month period, I decided to research afterlife connections. I thought, there must be a lot of people who have had experiences like mine. I had been having them my whole life, so I went online and started researching. I really didn't know what I was looking for to tell you the truth. First, I Googled and searched different topics relating to the subject. I found different names of mediums, psychics, seers, and so on. Next, I decided to look on the internet and find a book about the afterlife. (Don't ask me why) I picked a book titled, "Afterlife Communication, 16 Proven Methods, 85 True Accounts." The cover of the book had a picture of a little boy standing in a doorway at the top of some stairs waving his hand. I guess since I had lost a son this drew me to purchasing the book. The book was from the Academy for Spiritual and Consciousness Studies. The editor of the book was Dr. R Craig Hogan, Ph.D. I didn't know it at the time, but this book put my journey into an entirely different gear. I read the entire book in no time flat. I took particular interest in a chapter by Dr. Hogan. This chapter had an online course teaching you how to connect to the other side. As soon as I saw this I was on it. I took the course. The course worked, and I learned and used Dr. Hogan's techniques to connect to the other side. His techniques really helped a lot, and I still use them all the time today. I searched high and low for other books and found that, supposedly, the standard text for the subject was "Opening to Channel, How to Connect to Your Guide", by Roman and Packer. As soon as I saw *standard text* I knew that I wasn't alone on my journey. I thought there must be tons of people like me who are on the same journey. Of course I ordered and read the book right away. It was very good and I do recommend it.

Also in the book "Afterlife Communication" there was another author by the name of Suzanne Giesemann. I found her very interesting. She obviously had credibility and a fascinating story. She is the kind of author who when you are reading one of her books, you can't put it down. They really are that good. The first book of hers that I read was "Messages of Hope." I couldn't put it down. I read all of her books that were related to my search. I read, "The Priest and the Medium." It is about B. Anne Gehman, another medium, and her husband Wayne Knoll, Ph.D. I was on a mission. I was reading books about other mediums, and learning their techniques. Another book Suzanne co-authored that I read was "Where Two Worlds Meet, How to Develop Evidential Mediumship." This book was about the medium Janet Nohavec. It was like a textbook on how to become a medium. I had my yellow highlighter out and used it throughout the book.

I spent the next 18 months studying, meditating and connecting, reading books, and keeping a journal of most of my readings. "Readings" are what I call my channeling with Spirit. I wouldn't call it obsessed, but I literally couldn't get enough on the subject.

Over this period of time, I read over 30 books about the afterlife. I was like a student who loved their schoolwork and I learned a lot. I really believe you can learn a lot from other peoples' experiences and by reading books. A skeptic might say, "You can't learn how to do that kind of stuff from a book." I disagree. They use textbooks in school don't they? Well this library that I was amassing was my school and I loved it. Not only was I reading all the time, but I was also putting my gained knowledge to use in my readings about four times a week. It seemed that every time that I bought and read a book, it had one or two items in it that hit home with me big time. I would think, "Oh my gosh that has happened to me before!" "Wow, I have been doing that my whole life!", or "Whoa that just happened to me the other day!" I just couldn't get enough.

Wilma had changed my life. I almost felt like I had wasted 50 years. I think things do happen for a reason. Since my daughters were basically grown when the event with Wilma happened, I, for the first time in my life actually had time to spend on my gift. There was going to be no more hiding from it. I was embracing it for the first time in my life and I loved it. There was a whole other world out there to explore and I had on my hiking boots. I was on it. The next chapters in this book will have actual stories of my readings and their validations; but first I want to explain how I connect to the other side and what I have learned and believe.

I sit in a chair. I like to wear loose fitting, relaxing clothing. I wear ear muffs to drown out the noise (we live on a busy street). They are the kind of ear muffs that you would wear at a gun range. I start by closing my eyes and relaxing my body. I have found that if you relax your shoulders, it will help you relax the rest of your body. I slow down my breathing to where it is slower but still comfortable. I put my hands in my lap. Then in my mind, I state the following to prepare myself for the other side. "I am going to the place of love, unconditional love. I am protecting myself, my chair, my house, and my whole family with the white light of God, where nothing but high level, high minded spirits from the white light of God may enter, in Jesus' name, amen. God is the light, God is the everlasting light, and God is the everything. I am opening up all seven of my chakras, and clearing them, and letting the white light of God flow through my body. I am opening up my brow and crown chakras and going up through the white light of God like an antenna and seeking information from Spirit, the Book of Life, and the Akashic Records." I then ask for guidance from my spirit guides and guardian angels. I also ask for guidance and a connection to spirits that I have had contact with. I can't connect every time that I try, but I can usually connect with one of them or gain insight from my guides or guardian angels. This format has changed a few times over the last 18 months, but this is the one that I use and prefer right now. You have to use what works for you, and go with it. Notice, I always ask for information. I don't demand it. I don't think Spirit takes orders. I don't even know if I get my information from the Book of Life, and Akashic Records, but that is what I ask for, and it works for me.

When I do make a connection, this is how it works. They show me images. These images are sometimes just a fuzzy grey silhouette, sometimes they are in color. I do see color. Sometimes there is like a two second film clip that I am shown. Nothing is said verbally. It is done telepathically. Spirit puts thoughts into my mind. These thoughts are usually just for a split second, but tell a lot. I hear things, but they are done telepathically. I do hear things. I hear them out loud (in my mind). Sometimes they just convey a feeling or message to me that my mind understands. I can also feel their emotions (it seems when they want me to). I also use a notepad to take notes when I am in a reading. I do this because I found out if I don't take notes, I can't remember a lot of things from the reading. A lot of times they use symbols to convey a message. For the first year I didn't pick up on that very well. It took me a while to figure that out. I did buy a book called "Dream Images and Symbols" by Kevin J. Todeschi. It explains what a lot of symbols stand for. I told Spirit this (as if they didn't already know) and asked them to use some of these symbols. And yes, they have responded quite well.

When I do a reading, sometimes I am in a place of beauty where everything is beautiful and wonderful. Sometimes, I might be in a park with Spirit or sometimes at a playground. A lot of times I am just in another time and space of consciousness only. In this place I don't see much of anything around in the area. I just see and feel what they want me to know during the connection. That is why I call it a different time and space. But make no mistake, I am always in a place of love. It seems the more I use the word love in my readings, the better my connection can become. You see, in the afterlife, the most important thing is love and understanding. When I do my readings, I do them alone. I don't have a sitter with me. I know a reading is finishing up when I feel the energy from the spirits starting to fade. I ask my spirit guides, guardian angels, Wilma (who I believe is my main spirit guide), and other spirits that I have connected to, to connect me to spirits that I am trying to channel. So far, it has worked for me. Like I said before, I have to use what works for me.

Speaking of spirit guides, guardian angels, and even angels, yes there is such a thing. I don't see my guardian angels in human form, but I sense their presence. It seems that they are beings of light. They are always with you. They are there to help and protect you on the earth plane. When you get a feeling of intuition, I believe it is your guardian angel letting you know what to do. I'm sure there have been times in your life when you have had a gut feeling about something, didn't go with it, afterwards only wishing you had. Try going with your first instinct. It can have a huge impact on, and change, your life. It will also help train you to pick up on signs from the spirit world. The signs are always there, you just have to train yourself to recognize them. From my own experiences, it seems as if angels are pure beings of light. I believe they can take the form of a human, if they want or need to. I have seen angels in some of my readings. Sometimes they appear with wings and sometimes they are just a pure being of light. They seem to be high spiritual beings. They seem to be messengers of love and religion. I do actually see my spirit guides. I don't see them all the time, but I feel their presence when I do readings. They are actually there to give you guidance on events in your life and can connect you to other spirits on the other side. Spirit guides are there to help you. Now, as far as Jesus goes, I have seen Jesus in a lot of readings. I believe most of the time what I am seeing is Jesus being used as a symbol when Spirit is trying to get a religious message to me. In a couple of readings, I have seen Jesus standing, and in front of him will be a child sitting on the ground. This child is always captivated and in awe of Jesus in front of him or her. This is one way that Spirit lets me know that someone lost a child or sibling at an early age. There was one reading in particular where as soon as I connected to the other side I noticed that I was walking across sand dunes. I was following someone in a white robe. The robe had a hood on it and it was pulled over the head of this person. I was behind this person. He was leading me somewhere and I was following. I couldn't see his face. It felt good and right so I kept following. When we crested this one high hill of sand he let me catch up. Upon arriving at the top of the dune, and seeing this man for the first time, I realized it was Jesus. Here is my description of him. He had longish hair, not real long, but medium. He had a tanned looking face and skin. He wasn't real white and he wasn't real dark. He had a beard, but it was only scruffy, not long like you see in some pictures. He also had on sandals. Jesus didn't say anything to me. He raised his left arm showing me what was on the other side of the hill. As I looked, I was in awe. The best way for me to describe it is what I call, "The City of Light." I didn't see a bunch of lights, but in my mind, I heard those words, "The City of Light." This event happened right after I learned how to connect to the other side. It kind of startled me so my connection faded and that was the end of it. I will never forget it.

Okay, one last thing before we move on to actual readings and validations. This is about people who know me and what they think about my mediumship. Some of them believe what I do is real. There are so many validated readings, how could they not. To tell you the truth, I think it is harder to make validations to your friends and family than it is for someone else. I mean, you are all aware of the same stories. I can't tell my cousin this- Your dad says you loved to play softball. This is something that we both already knew. I did tell a close family relative that when she was looking up to the clouds, while on the beach, and on vacation, talking to her dad, he heard her. She said that she had done exactly that. So that is how you have to validate friends and family. There are people I know that are doubters and I really can't blame them. There are a lot of things written in this book that are hard to believe. Some people, on the other hand, simply don't agree with what I do. I respect their opinion; I really do. I am a person of faith. I have read the Bible and I have also been to heaven and back. Faith is a good thing. I hope these people keep their faith because I know where it will take them. *Remember, I have already been to where they ultimately hope to go. I have already been in the presence of God, Jesus, and angels. What an incredible journey it has been!*

CHAPTER SEVEN

Wilma Readings and Validations

This entire chapter has actual stories of readings that I have done. They have also been validated by one or more family members. These are true accounts with no exaggerations. As you will see, I have done a lot of readings for Wilma's girls. Their mother, Wilma, along with God, awoke me spiritually in October of 2014. You will also see how good of a connection I have with Wilma, simply by the number of readings and validation accounts that are listed herein. After my initial letters to the girls, I started doing readings for them around February of 2015. I started documenting my readings on a regular basis in March of 2015. I kept everything in a binder. I would take notes during the readings. Next I would type a letter about the readings. I would make two copies of the finished product, one for me and one for them. This is a very time consuming process, but I am glad that I did it or I wouldn't have documentation of my readings.

THE SNOWMAN

After a few readings in February of 2015, of which I have no notes or records, but had several hits, I started documenting my readings regularly in March. In any reading I try to have one "wow" factor. This is an item from a reading where the sitter (the person I am doing the reading for/ I actually have no sitter with me) knows this is a hit that I couldn't have known about. In March of 2015, in a reading with Wilma, I started trying to channel Albert (Wilma's husband). When I finally did connect with him, all I got was the image of a snowman. It had a long carrot nose and a scarf. I saw the snowman in color. It was kind of leaning backwards. I saw it very briefly, but very clearly.

At work the next day, anytime that I thought about the snowman in the reading, I could feel the presence of Spirit. This is when I started to learn that Spirit was telling me something was important, by giving me sense of presence. Not being able to get this snowman off my mind, and feeling presence, I sensed that it was important, so I texted Teresa. I told her about the snowman and its description. I told her that I didn't know if it meant anything or not, but there it was. I thought maybe she had a picture of them and their dad with a snowman or something. She later texted me back and said that she and her sisters had just been to his and Wilma's grave the previous day. At the grave they hung a stuffed snowman with a long carrot nose, scarf, and hat, in a tree, and said it was for their dad. There it was, the wow factor! Not only that, but I had channeled someone that I didn't even know. It was a first for me and it was big. I must admit, I didn't notice the hat, but the rest of the story was there and unbelievable.

HOPE

In that very first reading with Wilma, I saw a small child on her lap. At the time, I couldn't figure out who it was. I knew that Wilma's daughter Kathy had lost a child in childbirth. It was stillborn. It was a little girl and they named her Hope. It had just slipped my mind. In a reading in February I described a little girl that looked like

Kathy's other daughters. It then hit me who it was, it was Hope. I told Wilma's girls and they said that they had already figured that out. In a reading on March 2, 2015, I told Wilma's girls that I had seen Hope and she was walking hand in hand with Wilma and Ick (Albert's nickname was Ick, so that is what I will start calling him). They were showing me that Hope was with them and they were taking care of her. Kathy said that March 2nd was Hope's birthday! The same date that I saw her in a reading.

THE RING

A couple of months of readings had went by and Teresa and her sisters were wondering just how much information I could get. Of course, they didn't tell me this, but they had an event in mind. They were waiting to see if I said anything about it in a reading. On March 21, 2015, I did a reading. In it, I saw Wilma standing with Ick. She was holding a bouquet of flowers and had on a dress. She seemed very happy, as did Ick. As I looked at the two of them I noticed a ring on her ring finger. As I looked at it, it reflected very bright light. It reflected light like a car window does the sunlight; it was blinding. Obviously, this meant the ring had significance in the reading. This is when I learned that you have to tell a sitter everything you are feeling or getting. If you don't do it then, and it's a hit, then the wow factor isn't quite as high. After telling Teresa about the reading, she said that March 21st was her parents' anniversary! She and her sisters were waiting to see if I mentioned it. She couldn't believe it. Another unbelievable hit. I felt like the blinding ring meant their anniversary, but I didn't mention it. It didn't matter; the reading said it all. What a wow!

BOUNCING OFF THE WALLS

In another reading in March of 2015, I told Teresa that her mom was like I had never seen her before. She was giving off all kinds of energy. I told her that it seemed like she was bouncing off the walls. Teresa asked me what time I had done the reading. I told her and she said that she and her sisters were at Wilma and Ick's grave at that exact time. I think that says it all. Short story but very validating.

QUESTIONS

With so many good hits in such a short time, I thought that I should try and push myself even further. I told all four girls, Teresa, Kathy, Kelly, and Pam, to write down a question, seal it in an envelope, and ask Wilma and Ick that question every night for a week. I was not to know what the questions were. In late March, after about ten days, I really pushed myself hard in a reading, reaching high into the white light seeking answers to their questions.

Here were their questions. Teresa to her dad, Ick: what song were we singing in the car on my wedding day, on the way to church? Kathy to her dad, Ick: what was the last thing you said to me on the night of your passing to the other side? Kelly to her dad, Ick: she asked him something about a picture. Pam to her mom, Wilma: what did you use to say these things were, on my arm that were a result of me as a young child pulling a hot bowl of chili off the counter onto my arms? In a series of two or three readings in about a 10 day period that ended about 20 days after the beginning of the experiment, here were some of my notes. Keep in mind that I didn't know the questions. These notes were blind notes that at the time I had to assume were just messages in a reading for the girls. Here were my responses: I keep hearing the song "Chapel of Love." I was shown a drop of water. A window frame or picture, I can't tell which. Polka dots or dots. Keep in mind that I didn't have a clue to what their questions were. Seeing it now, the answers seem obvious, but at the time I didn't know what the questions were.

Teresa's question and answer are obvious. What song? "Chapel of Love." An exact hit.

Kathy's question, what was the last thing that you said to me on the night of your passing? At the time, Kathy was a teenager. She heard her dad get up in the night, and she asked him what he was doing. He said that the faucet water was dripping, and he had got up to turn it off. I said that I was shown a drop of water. Another exact hit. It doesn't get more exact than that.

Kelly's question was about a picture. In my notes I put "I am seeing either a window frame or a picture. I can't tell which one it is." I certainly would also call that a hit.

Pam's question, what did you use to say these things were, that were a result of me as a young child, pulling a hot bowl of chili off the counter onto my arms? The answer was "Spots." In my notes from the reading I put, "I am seeing polka dots or dots." This was pretty much another hit.

I know some skeptics would say that this experiment might have proved psychic abilities, but not mediumship. Call it what you want, but I answered all of their questions without ever seeing them. I considered it a huge success.

THE KEY AND THE DOG

In April of 2015, about the same time that I was finishing the previous envelope experiment, without my knowing, AJ and Shelby asked their grandmother, Wilma, a question. AJ and Shelby are Teresa's children. They were trying to see if I would pick up on the answers in any of my readings. AJ asked Wilma about a key on a chain that he threw to her in the living room one evening. It hit her in the face, injuring her. His question was, "What did I throw at you and hit you with?" In an April reading I mentioned seeing a key on a long chain. Shelby asked Wilma if her dog, who had passed away, was with her. In another reading in April I mentioned seeing a dog who licked me on the face. I described the dog, and yes, Shelby's question was answered. Her dog was on the other side with her grandparents.

LAUREN'S ENVELOPE

On May 17, 2015, I did a reading and in it I mentioned seeing Wilma standing alone holding an envelope. She was holding it in her hand. The envelope was facing long ways like an envelope usually would be seen. Obviously, this was significant, but I had no idea what it meant. So I logged it in my journal noting that I didn't know its significance. After Wilma's girls read my notes from this reading, Kathy, Wilma's daughter and Teresa's sister, quickly realized that the envelope and date had real significance. May 17th was the exact date that Kathy's daughter Lauren received her letter of acceptance to the nursing program at the university at which she had applied! She had been waiting on news from the university. Of course, I had no idea about this, but obviously Wilma did!

WEST SULLIVAN STREET

Okay, this is one of the most in depth readings that I have ever done. I really don't think that I have ever figured it out completely. In June of 2015, I was channeling Wilma. Keep in mind, when a medium gives you numbers that mean something, names that mean something, or descriptions of people that are correct, it doesn't get any better than that. There are many other ways to validate a reading, but these three are right at the top. Wilma gave me the name of a street. It was W. Sullivan Street. I also got the numbers 1, 3, and 6. After getting these numbers, I was told, "no, there are two 1's." At this point I had to assume that it meant the address was 1136 W. Sullivan Street. In this reading I also saw a little girl with dark hair. She was carrying a basket that was full of flower petals. She was taking the petals and throwing them on the ground as she skipped around. In the room, where she was skipping around, there was a dark haired man, who had a dark complexion, and was handsome. There was also a sandy-blonde, attractive woman, who was well manicured on the opposite side of the room. They didn't seem to notice the little girl skipping around. It seemed as if they were in a funeral parlor, attending a wake for the little girl, who I had to assume was their daughter.

I gave the notes from the reading to Wilma's girls. Upon reading them, Teresa said that W. Sullivan St. was where her mom grew up as a small child. The address of her childhood home was 1316 W. Sullivan Street. The same four numbers that I was given in the reading except I put them in a different order.

Remember, in the reading, I was told, "no, there are two 1's." I made the assumption that I was being told 1136, not 1316 or any other number. Anyway, you can see what I am getting at. I just inserted the second number 1 in the wrong place of the address. Or did I? The reason that I ask that is because Jennifer, my youngest daughter, Googled the address 1136 W. Sullivan Street. The result that she got just blew me away. Google had the address of 1136 W. Sullivan Street listed as "Heavenly Daycare." I just about came out of my seat. I think Wilma had me make that mistake on purpose. In this reading there was Wilma's childhood street and the numbers for the address of Wilma's childhood home. Wilma wanted to leave no doubt for her daughters that this was a message for them from her. If there still were any doubts, she wanted them erased.

After the validations from this amazing reading, I have never been able to figure out the little girl with the flower petals and her parents. Maybe I am just overlooking something. Or maybe there is a story there that I don't know about and someone will read my story and figure it out. There is always hope.

BROWN EYES

In June of 2015, I also did a reading on Wilma's girls' dad, Ick (Albert). In this reading he clearly showed me a set of brown eyes. They were looking right at me and were very large. It was an obvious message so I wrote it down in my notes. He also showed me a necklace that had a big piece on it. I couldn't tell what the piece was, but wrote it down in my notes from the reading. Wilma's girls said that their dad always called them his "brown eyed girls." They said he also always wore a necklace with a "horn of plenty" on it. Two short, but quick validations in this reading.

SHORT SHORTS

In July of 2015, during a reading I picked up on the name Jody. I told Teresa that I saw a young girl in her twenties. She had light colored hair, a nice complexion, long legs, and was tall and thin. She was also wearing short shorts. Teresa said that it was her cousin Jody. Jody died in an accident when she was in her twenties. She said the description fit her perfectly. Not only that, but Teresa said that she always wore short shorts. Here, we have her name, description, and short shorts in the reading. It just doesn't get any more validating than that.

KELLY'S DRILL

In August of 2015, I did a reading with Wilma and Ick. During this reading, among other things, I was shown a wood boring drill bit. I was also shown an image of Kelly (Teresa's sister, and Wilma's daughter). This is one of those items you get in a reading and you think, "A wood boring drill bit?" That can't mean anything. Should I even write it down in my notes? I have learned from experience that the smallest little detail can be the "wow" factor in a reading. Sometimes it turns out to be nothing and other times it turns out to be everything. After Kelly read my notes from the reading, she quickly realized that it was significant. On August 30th, Kelly was doing maintenance at the complex where she worked; this was her job. She was a maintenance person for an apartment complex. On this date she had a tenant that needed their locks changed on the doors. Kelly was kind of reluctant to do this job. She was always uneasy about doing a job for people that she didn't know. She carried out her duties as the maintenance person and finished the job. In doing the job, Kelly had to use a wood boring drill bit. This was on the exact day that I did the reading. To this day, Kelly knows that it was a message from her mom and dad that they were with her and protecting her.

THE LAWN CHAIR

On August 2, 2015, I did a reading with Wilma. I was shown an image of Teresa sitting in a lawn chair. I wrote down in my notes that the chair was red and black. Standing beside Teresa was Wilma. I wrote down exactly what I was shown, Teresa sitting in a red and black chair with Wilma standing next to her. I also noted in the reading how upbeat Wilma seemed to be. After reading my notes, Teresa said that she had been sitting in a red and black lawn chair that weekend, with her sisters, in her backyard. She said that a song came on the radio which was upbeat, and she mentioned to her sisters that their mom would love that song. This wasn't exactly a "wow" reading, but very worth mentioning.

THE TWO SONGS

Every once in a while I will ask Spirit to step up for me and give me even better validating evidence than I had been getting. Notice I said asked, not told. I really don't think you can tell Spirit anything. That is why I always ask and not demand anything from Spirit. So in August of 2015, I did just that. I asked Spirit to give me some validations that would just blow us away. On August 2nd, I did a reading with Wilma and Ick. In this reading, I again got the song "Chapel of Love" from Ick. I didn't think much about it; I wasn't seeing anything that would be a "wow" factor. Also, in a reading with Wilma in August, I put down in my notes that I was shown a rose lying on the night stand next to a bed. I gave this information to Teresa and really didn't think much of it. Obviously, Teresa picked up on "Chapel of Love" coming from her dad, Ick. After a couple of days went by, Teresa texted me at work and said that her mom, Wilma, had heard the song, "The Rose" right after her dad, Ick, had passed. She was lying in bed one night and heard the song coming from what sounded like a music box which she didn't own. At this point, we still didn't put it together. Then while working the assembly line it hit me. Both of the spirits that I had been channeling gave us a message. They both responded with a song. Sometimes you can't see the forest because of the trees. This was the better than average validation that I had asked Spirit for and had now received it. As soon as I went on break, I texted Teresa and told her about the two songs. It just blew us away. I again texted her to ask her something and I will never in my life forget her response. She said she would get back to me shortly because I had just totally blown her mind! Little did she know that my mind had also been blown. I will never forget that response of hers as long as I live. It makes me laugh out loud and tear up at the same time because I was feeling the same energy as she was.

PAM'S BIRTHDAY

With all the hits that I was getting doing readings, I decided that I wanted to push harder. I wanted a "wow" that was just simply undeniable. At the beginning of October, 2015, I asked Spirit to give me some physical signs. I asked for electronic signs, physical signs, anything that they could give me for validations. It didn't take long before I had got what I asked for. Our main large screen television set came on by itself six times. Yes, not once, but six times. It had never done that before I asked for a sign. Barb and I also heard a door slam shut inside our house in the middle of the night. Also, Barb felt someone touch her while lying in bed, not once but twice. Barb also felt someone sit down next to her in bed; she felt the bed compress. Also, on the night of October 9th, 2015, while I was getting ready for work at 4:30 am, something else happened. I had slept with a box fan on Barb's dresser next to the bed. It was tilted slightly backwards up against the dresser mirror. While getting ready, I tip toed past the bed to get my phone which was sitting on the nightstand next to the bed. As I went past the bed, the fan tipped forward, not backwards, but forwards. As it did so I just happened to catch it. I tried to re-create or debunk this, but I couldn't get it to fall forward. I could get it to stand upright by jumping up and down on the floor, but not tip forward. Obviously, I was hearing Spirit loud and clear and so were Barb and my daughter, Jennifer. They were starting to get a little spooked so I asked Spirit to stop with the physical signs. None of these things ever happened again after I asked Spirit to stop. I thought that was the end of the story, but it took a bit of a twist a week later. I mentioned what had happened on the night of October 9th, to Teresa. She said that October 9th was her sister, Pam's, birthday. At Pam's house on the night of October 9th, Pam said she had felt her mother's presence in her room in the middle of the night. She said that she couldn't see her but she knew she was there. Pam said that she had told nobody about the event except her sisters so there is no way that I could have known. Also on that same night, Kathy (one of Wilma's girls) said that her doorbell rang in the middle of the night. So here it was, I had gotten the "simply undeniable wow" that I had asked for and didn't even know about part of it until after the fact. An unbelievable, but true story. Happy Birthday Pam!

THE MILITARY PIN

On November 3rd, 2015, I did a reading with Wilma and Ick. In this reading I saw and described a military pin that Ick was wearing. A day or two later, Teresa posted a picture of Ick with his mother on Facebook. He was wearing a military uniform which also had a military pin attached to it. I had this information written down in my notes, but had not yet given the notes to Wilma's girls. So this was only a validation for me. I mention this story so that you understand this is one of the downfalls of doing my readings alone. It actually happens quite often. I will get information in a reading, put it in my notes and journal, before giving the information to the sitter, and the validation happens in that time frame. It is a good validation for me, but not really for the sitter because they could just easily assume that I wrote down the notes after their event happened. Very understandable.

THE ANGEL

In a reading with Wilma on December 8, 2015, she was letting me know that there was a special tree topper. It was the Christmas season and Wilma, Ick, and Wilma's girls loved Christmas. I didn't know what she meant by this message of a "special tree topper", but I passed it along to the girls. Come to find out, Kathy had put an angel on the top of her Christmas tree that used to be Wilma's. This wasn't an every year thing, it was something that she just happened to do that year. Merry Christmas Kathy!

THE BADGE

In the same reading on December 8, 2015, I was shown a star. I didn't really think much of it so I jotted it down in my notes. In another reading on December 15, 2015, with Wilma and Ick, I was shown the star again. This time I tried looking further, to look for and find details. After looking further, I noticed that it wasn't a star, it was a badge. I knew that my nephew AJ was wanting to be a police officer, so I told his mother, Teresa, about the reading. On December 15, the exact date of my reading, AJ received a letter from the law enforcement agency which he had applied at, giving him information that he was waiting for. That is just plain crazy!

TYLER

In a reading on January 23, 2016, Wilma showed me an image of her grandson, Tyler. I didn't get much information on this, but knew that Tyler was on Wilma's mind, or she wouldn't have shown me an image of him. After talking to Pam, Tyler's mom, I found out that he was getting a few medical tests done which turned out good. A short story, but worth mentioning. It just shows that Spirit is in tune with our everyday lives whether we realize it or not.

BALANCE

In a reading on February 12, 2016, with Wilma and Ick, one of the messages that I got was from Ick. All he did was mention the word, "balance." Of course, I didn't think much about it, especially when I didn't hear back from Wilma's girls.

Keep in mind, this story is about the word "balance." I did a few other readings in early February. In these readings I put down in my notes the following: the horn of plenty, a star or badge, the colors red, blue, pink, and yellow, and the number 11. A couple of these rang a bell with Wilma's girls, and a couple of them didn't.

On February 14, 2016, I was at my desk shuffling my tarot cards. While shuffling them, one of them fell out of the deck and landed on the ground. I picked it up, and it was a major arcana card. I looked at it, and the card had the word "*balance*" on it! I just about hit the ground myself! Not only was it the "balance" card, it had the number 11 on it. It had a symbol that could be taken as a star or badge and it had a long holster type bag on it that could be taken as the horn of plenty. It had the colors red, blue, pink, and yellow, on it. This story still blows me away today. I wouldn't believe it myself if I didn't know it to be true!

I know this is the first time that I have mentioned tarot cards in this book. I picked up a set with a booklet on the internet. I did it just out of curiosity. I am glad that I did. These cards really do go along with everything that I have been studying. I don't use them a lot, but I do dabble with them every so often. Remember, keep an open mind as long as what you do is in the white light of God.

VALENTINE'S

On February 14, 2016, I also did another reading with Wilma and Ick. In this reading I was shown an eagle. I was also shown an image of Wilma and Ick sitting together on a couch. I really didn't think much of it at the time because it just didn't seem like much validating information. While I was typing up my notes from the reading, I looked at my symbols dictionary. Back in 2015, I bought the book, "Dream Images and Symbols", by Kevin J. Todeschi. I mentioned earlier in this book that I had asked Spirit to start using these symbols and it would help me decipher a lot of messages. It worked like a charm. I did find though that they were already using a lot of these symbols in my readings. I just didn't recognize them at the time. I looked up "Eagle." One of the meanings of an eagle in symbolism is the fourth chakra known as the heart chakra (chakra's are the energy points in the body). Well, that just blew me away. It was Valentine's! I also looked up two people sitting on a couch. It showed that this could be symbolism for a "love seat." Are you kidding me? Another Valentine's message! I just couldn't believe it. Happy Valentine's Day to Wilma's Girls!

BIRDS AND THE BEES

In March of 2016, I did another reading with Wilma. In it, I heard her say the phrase, "The birds and the bees and the flowers and the trees." I didn't bother to write it down. I thought maybe my mind was playing tricks on me or something. Sometimes in a reading, I see or hear things which I think couldn't be important, or even real. I sometimes have doubts about these things and am reluctant to pass the information along. You sometimes feel plain silly passing some information along. After I heard Wilma say it a second time, I decided to write it down and pass it along to Wilma's girls. After the girls read my notes, the two oldest girls, Kathy and Teresa, said their mom used to say it all the time when they were little. The younger girls, Kelly and Pam, didn't remember it; they were too young. A short message but a decent validation.

LINDSEY

I will mention just this one more Wilma reading before I move on. I have plenty more Wilma validations but there is no sense in listing all of them. I think that Wilma has made her point by now. Lindsey kept coming up in my readings with Wilma and Ick over a couple of months in 2016. It took me a while to figure out why. Lindsey is Wilma and Ick's first grandchild to graduate from High School, since I started doing the readings. They were just wanting her to know that they were with her in these important times of her life.

In a reading on March 29, 2016, with Ick, I was shown long dangling earrings. I was also shown the shape of a teardrop. I had never seen either one of these images in a reading so I wrote them down in my notes. The next day, Lindsey posted a picture of herself on Facebook wearing none other than a pair of long dangling earrings shaped like teardrops. It just flat blew me away! The downer was that I hadn't passed the information along to Wilma's girls yet. Lindsey is the youngest daughter of Kathy. I did text Kathy and tell her, but it was a little late for the "wow" factor.

In another reading on April 13, 2016, with Wilma, I was again shown Lindsey. This time I was shown a graduation robe with something significant around the collar. In my notes from the reading this is my quote, "All I got in this reading was a graduation robe. It had significance around the collar. I don't know if Wilma was symbolizing a medal or if the robe just had a wide hemming around the collar." This time I had already given the notes to Wilma's girls. A couple of days later, Kathy posted a picture of Lindsey on Facebook. In this picture, she was holding a medal that she had won that week. This medal was an award in honor of finishing in the top 10 percent of her class. This time we got the "wow" factor. Happy graduation Lindsey from grandma and grandpa!

Every story in this chapter is the exact truth, with no exaggerations. A few tears were shed by me and Wilma's girls with these readings, but they were all tears of joy! Wilma, I can't thank you enough. You brought me home to God on that October night in 2014. You are an amazing soul. I hope to continue connecting with you while I am here on the earth plane, and after that, for eternity.

CHAPTER EIGHT

Other Validations

OLD FRIENDS

In March of 2015, I had just started connecting to the other side. I was very inexperienced and really didn't know what to expect. In one of my very first readings that I ever did, after learning to make the connection, something very strange happened. I was standing in a large corridor. I looked to my left and there was a large room with an adjoining door. Inside this room were a lot of souls. They were all looking at me. It was kind of like I was new around here and they all knew it, and wanted to get a good look at me. At one point, I started realizing that some of those souls were my relatives. At about the same time, two people came out of nowhere. They approached me and I quickly realized that it was two guys that I went to high school with. They both had passed to the other side at an early age. They wanted to let their families know they were all right. It totally caught me off guard. I greeted them and said hello and I quickly moved on, leaving the room and corridor behind. I hadn't thought about those two guys in years and they were two of the first people on the other side to greet me. It really caught me off guard. I have seen them in another reading since then and they both still had the same message. They want their families to know that they are fine. I am now in the process of passing that message along. I am careful in approaching their families. Put yourself in the shoes of their family members. What would you do if someone came and told you that your dead family member said hello?!

MOTHER'S DAY

I did a reading with Barb's dad, on Mother's Day of 2015. Barb, my wife, grew up on a 110 acre farm. Her dad, in his line of work, was a maintenance man. Her mom was a bookkeeper by trade. Her mom is still with us today and she is a wonderful person. Barb was fortunate enough to come from a good family. In her early years, times were tough. Barb and her siblings wore homemade clothes and hand me downs. Times did get better for them in their teenage years when their parents made a good, middle class living. In my reading with Barb's dad, I was shown a bracelet. It was on his wife, Barb's mom's arm. He made references to it more than once. I knew that it was important. I wrote it down in my notes. A lot of times when I finish a reading, I can just tell when something important was in it, or if it was just a very good reading. After this reading, I sensed that importance. I asked Barb if her mom had a bracelet that she wore that was special. Barb said no. She said that her mom didn't wear bracelets. I had been around her family for decades and couldn't remember one either. I thought that I had a misread and screwed up in my reading. I went on with my business and that was that, or so I thought. About an hour later, Barb told me that her mom did have a bracelet that her dad had given her mom when they were kids. She said that her mom hadn't wore it in decades. Afterwards, Barb asked her mom about the bracelet. She told her that he had given her a charm bracelet as a gift, when the kids were small. She said that she hadn't wore it in years and it was piled in her jewelry box. It was a charm bracelet with a charm for each kid. It also had a charm for her on it. Here is the kicker of the story. Barb's dad had given her mom the charm bracelet, as a gift, decades earlier on Mother's Day! I can't think of a better way to validate to your family that you are still around, than this. Barb's dad hit this one out of the park! What a wonderful Mother's Day gift from him to his whole family. Happy Mother's Day to the entire family!

JESUS AND THE CHILD

I did a reading with Barb's dad, on October 25, 2015. In this reading I was shown a small child sitting in front of Jesus. Here is my description, in the reading, "A small child sitting in front of Jesus. This child was in awe. Jesus had his hands down to his side, palms open, with healing light coming from behind him." Usually when I see a small child in a reading, it is a symbol that someone lost a child or sibling who passed while young. I wrote this down in my notes not really thinking a lot about it. Barb's mom later told her that her dad's sister, Sharon, had a twin when she was born who didn't make it. This certainly was news to me, but another exceptional validation from her dad. Also very heartwarming for Sharon, knowing that her sibling was with her brother, the rest of her family, and more importantly, with Jesus. Barb's dad just kept hitting them out of the park!

FAMILY FRIEND

On November 18, 2015, I did a reading and an old family friend stepped forward. She was very close to the family before she passed to the other side. As in any reading, I asked for validating information. In doing so, she showed me a Bible with a special page saver shaped like a cross. I wrote this information down in my notes and left it at that. I hadn't really been around her children, except

49

for a few family parties over a period of time between 30 or 40 years, so I didn't contact them about the reading.

In another reading, on March 13, 2016, she appeared again. This time she just flat out stepped forward. She was getting my attention. She showed me a couple of symbols. I didn't know what they were, but I drew them on my notepad. Like any reading, I sit in a chair in my bedroom with the door locked so that I am not disturbed. I also wear my ear muffs to block out any noise. I usually only do readings when I am the only one home or just me and Barb are home. During this particular reading, all at once, out of nowhere, I smelled a very strong odor of perfume. It was unmistakable. I thought maybe somehow Barb had unlocked the door and gotten into the bedroom. Of course, my eyes were closed so I couldn't see what was in front of me. I knew someone was either standing in front of me or had just walked past me. The person was wearing perfume. Upon opening my eyes nobody was there. I walked over to the closet, and looked inside. Nobody was there. I went out to the hallway looking for Barb. She was in the shower and the bathroom door was closed. I asked her if she had been in the bedroom while I was meditating and she said no. She had been in the bathroom the entire time that I was in the bedroom doing my reading. Nobody had been in that bedroom except me and this family friend. By this time I had done over 200 readings and I had never had this happen. I don't ever remember smelling perfume in any reading. I knew she was wanting this message passed on to her kids, but like I said, I hadn't been around them in decades. After a couple of weeks went by, I decided to roll the dice, and contact one of her children. It was one of her daughters. I sent her a message on Facebook, not knowing what to expect as her response. As usual, in a case like this, I will say something, and if the person doesn't warm up to me, I let it go. If they respond with sincerity, and/or honest curiosity, I will tell them everything that I know. Her daughter did show that genuine honest curiosity, so I told her everything that I had from my readings. I even mentioned the smell of flowers to her. This went along with the smell of perfume in the reading. Her response, "wow." Her mother did have a special Bible that had a cross shaped page saver. She said that she also always wore a very strong smelling perfume. She said that her mother was always out in the yard planting flowers. She didn't know about the symbols, but everything else really hit home. I have to rank this validated reading up there pretty high, especially with the smell of perfume right in front of me in the reading room!

LASSIE

Also in the previously mentioned reading on November 16, 2015, I saw our family member, Lassie. Lassie was our Collie that had passed to the other side about four years earlier. I mentioned this to Barb and she said that November 16th was Lassie's birthday! I didn't know this. I'm sorry, but I just can't keep up with these kind of dates. A great validation for me though. Thank you Lassie, we love and miss you!

KS

In early 2016, I noticed that Suzanne Giesemann was doing seminars throughout the summer. I was toying around with the idea of going to one of them. Barb and I talked about it a little, but didn't commit to anything. We are middle class and if we do something extra like that, it would basically be counted as our vacation.

In a reading with my dad on February 21, 2016, I was shown the letters KS. I didn't have any idea what they meant but I wrote them down in my notes. Later, when reviewing my notes, and thinking about the reading it hit me like a brick wall. I mean, what else could it have meant? I had been looking at a Suzanne Giesemann event that was going to be out in the Kansas area. Having learned to listen to my intuition and especially my dad in a reading, I booked this

Suzanne Giesemann event right away. I had read all of her great books about mediumship and I wasn't going to let this opportunity slip past me. Right after I booked us for this Suzanne Giesemann event which was in June of 2016, another one of her events was announced for September of 2016, in Missouri. After asking Barb for permission to buy tickets to this event, I booked it. We had both events booked and were committed. Our kids were now grown. It was time for us to do a few things on our own. We had always taken only family vacations; it was time. Hey, that's what happens when you start getting old. Barb was onboard. We could get some time on our own to just relax, and at the same time, maybe learn something valuable.

Right after making our plans to go to the Suzanne Giesemann events, I asked Spirit if I made the right decision. A lot of times I will ask Spirit questions or seek advice in a reading. Every day when driving to work at 4:50 am, I speak to Spirit during my 25 mile commute. I will speak out loud in the car not looking for a response, just talking. On March 7, 2016, while making my morning commute, I asked Spirit if I made the right decision booking the Giesemann events. When I say I ask Spirit, it means that I am asking my spirit guides, guardian angels, and all other spirits that I have regular contact with for advice. On this particular morning I asked for three signs throughout the day to validate me making the right decision. I asked for a *pig* sign. Don't ask me why, but that is what came to my mind. I asked for an *American Flag* sign. I also asked for a third sign of which I did not specify, only asking that I would recognize it. As soon as I finished making my "3 sign request", I turned on the car radio. The very first word spoken was "Joshua." I couldn't believe it. I had been doing readings for a friend, with a son named Joshua that were very in depth. Joshua will come up again later in this book. While still in the car, right after my request, I already had my third sign. Unbelievable 1! Later that morning, while listening to the radio at work, working the assembly line, Unbelievable 2 happened. The morning show radio host did a story about a pig! I couldn't believe it. A little later that day a maintenance buggy drove past my work area. On the back of it was an American Flag flying. This was not real uncommon at work, but you didn't see it all the time. Unbelievable 3! I had received all three signs that I asked for in no time flat. I think Barb and I did make the right decision. Thank you, Dad, and thank you Spirit.

CHAPTER NINE

Intuition, Guides, Guardian Angels, and other Stories

In this chapter, I will briefly go through a few stories. These stories are to show that the signs and messages are there, you just have to look for them. I believe that these signs and messages can come from your Spirit Guides, Guardian Angels, and intuition. Maybe even God and Jesus. You just have to learn how to tune in and listen.

In May of 2015, I asked my son, David, who is on the other side, to give me some signs through Madison, our granddaughter. Just a few days later, Madison, who was four years old at the time, was downstairs at our house with our daughter, Jennifer. While downstairs with Jennifer, Madison asked who those other people were that were standing down there. Obviously, there weren't any other people with them. At least not the kind that a person would usually see. Jennifer said that her whole body got the cold chills and they came right back up the steps. Madison had never mentioned anything like that before. This was the first time, and it was just a couple days after I asked for the signs from David. Of course, Madison knew nothing about my request to David. Another night in the summer of 2015, Madison was again playing with her Aunt Jennifer. They were in the spare bedroom which was now our toy room. While playing with dolls, Madison, as she looked down the hallway, asked Jennifer if they could play somewhere else, where nobody was watching them. Did she really see people standing there? I guess I will probably never know for sure, but I would have to say yes. When I do question Madison about these events, I do it very soft and easy. I don't want to make her afraid to talk about it. Whenever I do ask her about it, she kind of shies away from any questions. As she gets older, maybe she will open up more about it. I am just trying to make sure she understands, at an early age, that this kind of stuff is okay to talk about. Madison does talk about ghosts standing at the foot of her bed at night. She says that it scares her. Does Madison see these spirits? Is she tuned in with the other side? I think maybe she is. Now she does watch some television shows about the paranormal with me. I have also taught her how to sage (Saging is a ritual of burning white sage leaves to cleanse the energy in a specific area) the house like I learned from reading Theresa Caputo's books. When you read one of her books, it is like she is standing there talking to you. They are definitely in her dialogue. Madison has even sat in on an investigation with Jennifer and me, where we did an EVP session and used an EMF device (these are electronic devices used to pick up on energy sources). So yes, some of her ideas may be coming from these experiences with me, but seeing all these spirits that she mentioned happened before we did any of those exercises. In early 2016, Madison told me that our dog "Lexi", was outside next to the barn where the chickens used to be kept. That really caught my attention because that did used to be a chicken barn about 40 years ago. The previous owner told me that 20 years ago when we first bought the place. How would Madison know that? I had never mentioned it to her. So yes, I think that people can tune in to the other side, especially children. These young children haven't been taught to tune out their abilities yet. They tell you what they see at this age. Will this be the end of it for Madison? I hope not. Only time will tell....

In June of 2015, it was one of those days where we were just doing little things and hanging out in the house for a few hours. I noticed as I walked through the living room that Barb and Jennifer were going through all of our old videos. I thought nothing about it and said or asked nothing. I went on with my business of going through some old paper work that was in a small safe downstairs. As I was finishing up, I started to close the small safe door. It wouldn't close. Every time I tried to close the safe door, me and Barb's wedding video kept falling out. It did this three or four times. It wouldn't stay in the safe. I didn't add anything to the safe so it wasn't any more crowded than before I started on this project. I had never had this problem with the video before. After about four attempts of trying to close the door, I gave up. I took the video out of the safe, took it upstairs and laid it on the kitchen counter. A few hours later, Barb asked me what that video was doing lying on the kitchen counter. I explained what had happened with the safe. She told me that she and Jennifer were out in the living room going through all the old videos looking for our wedding video. We both recognized right away that Spirit was lending us a helping hand!

In August of 2015, I went jogging. I am a big guy, but every once in a while I will go for a short two or three mile jog. I will admit though, when you get into your fifties, it does take a toll on your body more than it used to. During my jog, I told Spirit that I was going to make God and Jesus a bigger part of my mediumship. I told Spirit that my readings would be leaning a little more towards the Godly side. I no more than said this and three yellow butterflies flew around and circled me. Yes, not one, but three! They came out of nowhere. It was a quick, wonderful, message that I will never forget as long as I live.

It was September of 2015. I had been working so much overtime at work over the last several years that it was building up, making it hard for me to relax and get a good reading at times. I asked Spirit to give me something in my sleep. While sleeping one night in September, I had a dream. I dreamt that I had lost my cellphone. I had never dreamt about this before that night. That very morning, on my way to work, at 5:00 am, I got to a construction area where the lanes divided to single lanes. Each lane had concrete barriers, making it only one car width wide. Right before entering the barrier area, my intuition told me not to go behind this truck that was pulling a boat. Of course, I didn't listen to my guardian angel, and followed the truck into the barrier area. Next, I saw sparks flying everywhere and the truck came to a stop. The boat trailer had come loose from the truck that was pulling it. So here I am stuck on the highway in the dark. Luckily, an eighteen wheeler was behind me and he got the rest of the traffic to stop. The truck driver behind me got out and went to help the boat owner. I also got out of my car and went to help. After securing the boat trailer back onto the truck, the truck driver and myself got back into our vehicles and preceded to drive on. About a quarter mile down the road, I knew something didn't seem right. I always sat with my cellphone in my lap whenever I drove to work. It wasn't there. Panicking (you probably know the routine), I couldn't find my phone anywhere while trying to drive the interstate. Finally, I reached down and found it right by the door bottom. It barely stayed in the car! Instantly, I remembered the dream. I laughed out loud and knew Spirit was staying connected to me through all of this overtime. This particular story wasn't a huge wow, but it involved both my Guardian Angel, and Spirit connecting to me in a dream. That is why I mentioned it. Most of the time, if you look for signs, symbols, and messages, they are there. You just have to let your mind tune in. Besides, when things like this happen it mixes it up a little bit, and makes it fun. Spirituality can really be a lot of fun. Enjoy it every chance you get!

It was the November deer hunting season, in 2015. I was sitting in my hunting blind, relaxing and watching the woods when a thought entered my mind. I knew that it was my intuition trying to tell me something. I have spent countless hours in the woods. It does give me a lot of time to just let my mind relax. I deer hunt every year. It is "my time." It is the only couple of weeks every year that I do my thing, regardless. It is my time to unwind. I have been doing it every year since my first wife, Cathy, and son, David, passed to the other side. My intuition, or guardian angel, put a scenario in my mind, about what to do if a certain situation should arise during my hunt. This intuition, guardian angel, whatever you want to call it, let me know that if a nice buck came in on me, and the kill shot was blocked by a tree, to shoot it in the back. This would stun the deer long enough for me to take him down with the second shot. About two hours later, this exact scenario happened. I took a very nice buck, just the way I was prepared by Spirit to do. It doesn't sound like much of a story, but I will never forget it. I know some people will say, "I thought you were all about love. How can you kill an innocent animal?" Well, I am a meat eater. I eat meat every day. The way that I harvest my wild animals is probably more humane than a lot of slaughter houses. I believe God put them here for us. I also know that plants are living things. I can see an energy field around them just like I do an animal. So the way I look at it is, what's the difference? Don't get me wrong, every time that I harvest an animal, I thank Mother Earth.

As I have mentioned before, a lot of times I will have something come up in one of my books that was just in one of my readings or connected someway to recent events in my life. I will only mention one story about this and move on, but it is very worth mentioning. I was in the process of reading one of the many books that I have bought and read since 2014. The name of this book was "Imagine Heaven", by John Burke. First, how this story leads up to the book. Earlier in this book I gave a description of what Jesus looked like. I also mentioned "the City of Light." This is how I described the event earlier in this book, about Jesus, and the city of light. "He had longish hair, not real long, but medium. He had a tanned looking face and skin. He wasn't real white and he wasn't real dark. He had a beard, but it was only scruffy, not long like you see in some pictures. He also had on sandals. Jesus didn't say anything to me. He raised his left arm showing me what was on the other side of the hill. As I looked, I was in awe. The best way for me to describe it is what I call, THE CITY OF LIGHT." Okay, that is what I had put in this book. Every once in a while I will let Barb read what I have put in this book up to the point of where I stopped writing. On this particular day I stopped right at the end of the paragraph that I just quoted. As Barb was reading my book up to the stopping point, I grabbed "Imagine Heaven", and began to read. There was a story from a person who had a near death experience and saw Jesus and the city of light. The description of Jesus's hair, beard, and robe, were right on with mine. Also this person described how Jesus directed him to look to his left, just as I had mentioned how Jesus raised his left arm. I let Barb read from the book just as I had, and she was just speechless. She had basically read the same description of Jesus coming straight from one of my readings. It was a good night. Barb and I both felt Spirit that night.

This next story is not mine. It is Teresa, Wilma's daughter's, story. I could not leave it out of this book. It is too good and also very true. My wife, Barb, has an Uncle who has Down syndrome; his name is Steve. He is her mom's brother. I call him the Rain Man. I do this because Steve remembers everybody's birthday. He knows everybody's birthday well out into all branches of the family. Of course, I am referring to the Tom Cruise, Dustin Hoffman movie, *Rain Man*. In the movie, Raymond (Dustin Hoffman) was good with numbers. If you remember the toothpick incident where they all fell on the ground and Raymond knew how many toothpicks fell, to the exact number. Just like *Rain Man*, Steve might have the mind of a child or other abnormalities, but he also has other special gifts that other people don't have. Steve is a kind, gentle person who is always smiling. He was in his mid-fifties when this story happened just a couple of years ago. Teresa, who is my sister-in-law, was up at my mother-in-law's house. While she was there, Steve also happened to be there. Steve was sitting in the living room watching television as he does quite often. Teresa walked into the living room where Steve was sitting. Steve started smiling and told Teresa that her friend Lily was very nice. Teresa asked Steve what he was talking about. Steve then told her that Lily was standing right next to her and she was a very nice lady. Of course, nobody was in the room except Teresa and Steve. By nobody, I mean nobody that a person would usually see unless they were tuned in to the other side. Steve's statement really caught Teresa's attention. Teresa has a relative named Lily who had already passed to the other side. Obviously, Teresa was not going to let this story stop here. The next time that Teresa was around Steve, she brought a picture of Lily. In that picture Lily was with several other women. She showed the picture to Steve and asked him to point out who Lily was. Steve did just that with no hesitation and on the very first try. I might add that Steve was wearing that smile as he did so. I know there have been some awesome stories and validations in this book that are my own personal experiences, but this story might be the best one in the book as far as I am concerned. Hey, I tell it like it is. Try to beat that story. Just like my granddaughter, Madison, Steve has an unspoiled mind. By this I mean that I think children's minds are capable of almost anything if they are not boxed in with perimeters. Also people who have certain disabilities in their lives, like Steve, can develop other parts of their psyche better than average people. Thank you for this story Teresa and Steve, and especially Lily!

In this picture of Steve you can tell he is different from most people by looking at him. Maybe he thinks the same as he looks at us. He is very happy in his world. He could probably teach us a lot if given the chance.

CHAPTER TEN

Joshua

Joshua and his family, while on vacation. Joshua passed just 2 months after this photo was taken. Back row: Marty, Lisa, Tom, Janet, Alisha, Kelly, and Eddie. Front row: Kyle, Josh, Ashlee, and Victoria. Josh's brother, Dylan, was not yet born.

This story is one that is very close to my heart. I went to high school with Joshua's parents, Marty and Lisa. Barb and I also worked with Lisa. We all worked together at the same grocery store; the very same store where Lisa insisted that I ask Barb out for a date. It is odd how things come complete circle sometimes. The average person would call it coincidence; I call it a long term form of synchronicity. At this particular store, I was a manager, Barb was an office manager, and Lisa was the scan/computer manager. Of course, Lisa was around when I lost my first wife, Cathy, and my son, David. Over time, Barb and I moved on and left the store. Lisa followed suit and left not too long after we did. Sometime after we separated from our lives together with Lisa at the store, we received terrible news. We found out that Marty and Lisa's son, Joshua, had lost his battle with cancer. Barb and I went to Joshua's showing at the funeral home. As we waited our turn in line to give our condolences to Marty and Lisa, I could feel the emotion building up inside me. After briefly speaking to Marty and Lisa we moved past the casket where Joshua lay. That is where I broke down and cried. I was not one to show my emotion. I couldn't help it; I felt their pain. Only someone who has lost a child can understand that kind of pain. Some people might think they can relate to a situation like that, but unless you've been there and done that, you don't know. I was now forever bonded with Marty and Lisa. We shared a common bond. Not a good one, but a bond nonetheless. I knew how big of a hole was in their hearts. Years went by, then decades passed. Barb and I hadn't heard from or seen Marty and Lisa in ages. You know how when you are busy raising your family, sometimes you just lose contact with friends. That is exactly what happened. After those twenty plus years of no contact, Barb and I became friends with Lisa on Facebook. We didn't message each other or even really correspond, but we at least had again made contact.

In early 2015, after learning how to make and initiate contact with the other side, I asked all my spirit friends and my son, David, to help me reconnect children with their parents. Being a person who had lost a child, I knew how much healing could come from a reading with a lost child. I had been there and done that with my own son, David. I will touch on that again in the next chapter. I really didn't know if my request would be realized or not, but I knew that I was going to try. I told Spirit that I wanted to dedicate the rest of my life to helping other people reconnect with lost loved ones, especially children. I knew exactly how those parents felt, and I knew that I could ease their pain if given the chance. I also mentioned to Spirit that I knew Marty and Lisa and that they had lost their son, Joshua. As if they didn't already know. I really didn't think a lot about it after making my request.

Shortly thereafter in a reading, I was shown Joshua. It was an image that wasn't real clear; it was kind of fuzzy. It was one of those readings where I was shown things, but I got most of my information from thoughts being put into my mind. In this reading, Joshua told me to talk to his mother, Lisa. He told me if I referred to him as "Joshy" it would draw her attention. I thought, "I don't even see Lisa, how can I tell her something like that?" Two days later, Lisa posted a picture of Joshua on Facebook. Since I don't believe in coincidence, I figured it was a sign of this greater synchronicity story going on, so I messaged her. I asked her if she ever called Joshua, "Joshy." She said that she did. After her response of yes, I asked Lisa for her address. I told her that I wanted to send her a letter, and she gave me the address. I know that she really had to be perplexed about my request. She hadn't heard from me or Barb in over twenty years and here I was asking about her son and wanting her address so that I could send her a letter. You have to understand at this point how far out on a limb I was going by sending Lisa and Marty a letter. I figured they would most likely think I had a *screw loose* or something. Also there were only a handful of people who even knew about the spiritual side of my life. Just like before with Wilma, I didn't care. I had a message to pass on and that was exactly what I was going to do. If there was just a small chance that I could help someone reconnect with their child, I was going to try. I figured at this point in my life my kids were grown and my reputation really didn't matter to me as much as it used to. If people thought I was *off my rocker* that was fine with me. For the first time in my life I had that kind of freedom. I was going to take advantage of it. I wanted to help people heal. I knew the benefits of healing from my own experience.

In my letter to Lisa and Marty, I briefly explained how I had gotten messages throughout my life. I told them about how Joshua asked me to call him Joshy and the story that went along with it involving his picture on Facebook. I also told them that Joshy had come to me again in a reading. This time he was brought to me by my son, David. Joshy wanted them to know that he was fine. In the reading I was shown an image of a pair of dirty baseball pants sliding into one of the bases on a baseball field. The kind of pants that kids wore when playing on a baseball team. I knew how many kids played baseball so I didn't really consider it a good validating message. I thought maybe that the dirty pants were a symbol for Lisa and Marty showing that he liked to get dirty on the field and slide into base as often as he could. I just didn't know. As always, I just told what I was shown in a reading. That was all I could do. I mailed the letter to Lisa and Marty not knowing what to expect from them as a response.

About a week later, Lisa messaged me. Her response was, "wow." At first when reading her response I didn't know if that was a good wow, or a bad wow. I didn't know if it meant, "Wow that is incredible, I would love to know more" or if it meant, "Wow, are you nuts or something?" Luckily it was a good response. Lisa was excited about the letter. She said that when she posted Joshy's picture it was the eighteenth anniversary of his passing. She also said that the very same week was her birthday and that Joshy loved to play baseball. It was all starting to make sense to me now. The reading seemed to be pretty accurate. Her birthday and the anniversary of his passing meshing together with what I had in the reading seemed to go hand in hand. Lisa seemed to get it. Since I received a good response from Lisa I thought that I should send her another letter explaining in a little more detail about my process of doing a reading. I did just that. I told her and Marty how it all worked and that Joshy was in a wonderful place. I explained how I received my messages and gave them details of how it felt in the afterlife. In the second letter, I mentioned that I did another reading with Joshy. In the reading I was shown a baseball field. The pitcher's mound was in focus. It was as if I was standing on first base looking at the pitcher's mound. *I told her that baseball must have been Joshy's sport because I was getting such strong messages about it.* I didn't tell her I thought maybe Joshy was a pitcher on his baseball team or played the infield because I seemed to be on first base looking at the pitcher's mound. Lisa responded and told me baseball was his sport. She also told me if I ever got anymore messages from Joshy she would love to have them. She said that I had no idea of how much she appreciated the letters about the readings. In closing she asked me if Barb and I knew that Marty had ALS (Lou Gehrig's Disease). I told her that we did not know and were very sorry to hear that about Marty. I will mention here that I had no idea at the time that this disease was as deadly as it is. A little time went by and I started thinking about what Lisa said about Marty and Lou Gehrig's Disease. *It dawned on me that Lou Gehrig was a baseball player* so I Googled his name. I just about hit the floor when I read that he was a first baseman! Right then I knew that Joshy had hit one out of the park. Not a solo homerun, but a grand slam! Of course, I messaged Lisa and told her the story. It is hard to pass on information like that to someone who has a sick spouse but I knew that Lisa would want to know anything that I knew. Joshy had, in his own way, given me several validating messages for his mom and dad. It was March of 2015, and I figured that was probably the end of it. I couldn't have been more wrong.

' Every once in a while after these first readings, I would again connect and touch base (no pun intended) with Josh. As usual I would take notes of my readings and later put them in a typed format. Several months passed. I didn't want to push my readings onto Marty and Lisa so I just kept my data in my journal and left it alone. In the summer of 2015, I had a dream that involved Lisa. Listening to my intuition, I messaged her. I asked her if she was interested in receiving anymore readings. She said that she had just driven by my house the other day and wondered if I had any more information. She told me that she would love to have any information that I had. Lisa also told me that as she was responding to my message, Josh's favorite song came on the radio. This whole story about synchronicity was all coming together now, stronger than ever.

In a reading on May 3, 2015, Josh let me know that when he was with Lisa's mom, Janet, and Lisa's sister, Kelly, there was a lot of playfulness and laughter. Also in this reading, Josh took his hand and waved it over an image of Marty in the shape of a rainbow. ***While doing so, he put this thought into my mind, "I got this."*** I put the information into my notes. ***Only later would I realize how important this message really was.*** Lisa did confirm that Josh was all about playfulness and laughter with Janet and Kelly.

In a reading on June 6th, I mentioned for the second time that I was shown western wear and clothing. The kind of clothes that a cowboy would wear.

Also in the summer of 2015, in August, I was again shown western wear by Joshua in a reading. Josh also showed me the image of a star and the number 32. I wrote the information down in my notes not understanding what it meant. I thought maybe Josh liked to dress up like a cowboy as a young child. But a lot of children did that so it just didn't seem like a good validation to me. A few days later, Lisa posted a picture of Josh on Facebook wearing a cowboys' attire. As soon as I saw his picture I immediately understood the validating message that Josh was trying to pass along. Lisa said that he loved wearing this kind of clothing. I will admit though, I don't know what the number 32 represented. Another piece of the synchronicity puzzle put into place!

In a separate reading in that same month of August, Josh showed me a baseball. It must have had a special meaning to him because it was in a small plastic case, that was cube shaped, not much bigger than the baseball itself. Lisa told me that she still has that very same baseball in that very same cube-shaped plastic case. A very good validation from Josh to his whole family.

On September 7, 2015, I mentioned that Josh seemed to be with another child. When I see a child on the other side, it is a symbol to me that there was a child death, miscarriage, etc. I mentioned this to Lisa and asked her if maybe someone in her family had had a miscarriage or something similar happen. She told me that when her son, Kyle, was born, there was a sac that didn't fully develop, with him. This was a message from Josh that his sibling was with him, and doing very well I might add!

In November of 2015, my connection to Josh was getting stronger. The messages were more clear and precise. If any of Marty and Lisa's family were skeptical of the readings at this point, that skepticism would soon fade. All of the following validating messages were given to me in November and December of 2015. I was shown a star fish. I didn't think it would mean anything but wrote it down anyway. Lisa confirmed that Josh was really into starfish at the beach and fascinated by them. She said that it was a very big validation. On more than one occasion I mentioned hearing a prayer verse. I asked Lisa if this particular prayer meant anything to her. It was a class "A" validation. She said that she would recite that exact verse all the time when thinking about Josh. In more than one reading Josh showed me an older gentleman that he was with. He was a kind gentleman that wore a fishing type hat. I also mentioned that I was picking up on the names of Thomas and Theodore. I also wrote in my notes that I thought maybe this gentleman was Josh's grandfather. Josh was very happy about being with this gentleman and wanted that message passed along. After reading my notes, Lisa confirmed that Josh was named after his great grandpa, Thomas. He was Lisa's mother, Janet's father. Thomas was Josh's middle name. Lisa said that he was a kind man who sometimes wore a hat like the one that I described. This was a very big validation. The name was right, along with the description. As I have mentioned earlier in this book when you get a name correct in a reading, it doesn't get more validating than that. I mentioned in several readings that I was being shown a race track. I was shown flags that would be posted, the bleachers, the track, and so forth. I wrote in my notes that it was "some kind of horse racing." Lisa said that Marty loves horse racing. This was a clear message from Josh to his dad, Marty, saying hello! In one of these readings, I mentioned that Josh was showing me the sky and putting the thought of "someone in the family makes a living in the aviation field." I didn't really think much about it because I knew that Marty worked in that particular field. I thought that maybe I was just getting mixed signals and not really getting a clear message. As usual, the little things in a reading can sometimes mean a lot for validating information. Lisa told me that Josh's brother, Kyle, is an airplane mechanic! In a reading on November 15, 2015, I mentioned seeing, for the third time, a small brown and black dog. Lisa said that she and Marty have a small brown and black dog, just as I described. Just another small, but validating message from Josh. Also in another reading in December, I wrote down in my notes, "and again, I am seeing go karts or race cars." Lisa said that Josh had a go kart and they still have it today! In another reading during this time frame, I mentioned that Josh was telling me something about Marty's stomach. Not knowing what he meant, I put in my notes that maybe Marty had a stomach virus. After reading my notes, Lisa told me that during that very same week as my reading about Marty and his stomach, Marty had a feeding tube put into his stomach. This of course was due to the Lou Gehrig's disease that Marty was dealing with. A validation of course, but not the kind you like to talk about. Josh was letting Marty and Lisa know that he was aware of what was going on and was also around them.

In January of 2016 I did a reading with Josh. In it, I mentioned that Josh showed me someone in bed sick, with a group of people standing over him.

In a reading on February 4, 2016 I stated the following, "It seems to me that Josh is telling me that Marty's condition might have worsened lately. He is letting me feel a recent setback."

In a reading on February 9, 2016, I stated the following, "In this reading, Josh showed me someone he is with. This was a pretty clear image that Josh showed me. This soul was about a foot taller than Josh. *This soul looked like Marty in the face.* This soul didn't have dark hair like Lisa's. It was not blonde, but light colored and wavy. *It was 100% either Marty's child or on Marty's side of the family. This soul was tall and thin (he really reminded me of Marty). He was a teenager.* This really stuck with me. *There is something very important about this reading.* This was a strong message that Josh is sending. *He is very happy about this person he is with. Josh has a very strong attachment to this soul that he is with.* I have to tell you, when I do a reading and something sticks with me like this, it really tells me that it is important information that Josh wants me and you to know. On top of that, as I type this paper my 6th chakra is swirling, almost making me dizzy. This is the third eye, or brow chakra. It has to do with intuitiveness. *That is a validation for me that what I'm reporting to you is either very significant, and/or, accurate."* I knew that this reading was very important, but I just couldn't figure out what Josh was trying to tell his family. The importance of this reading and the three previous readings was really weighing heavily on my mind; it wouldn't go away. Just like when it all first started with Wilma, I knew that this meant it was very important. I just couldn't put it together.

When Barb and I were out riding around town doing things, I kept telling her that something wasn't right. I told her that Josh was trying to tell me something to pass on to his family and I couldn't figure out what it was. I also told her that I had a really bad feeling about Marty and his health. That very evening I saw a post on Facebook by a friend from high school. In the post, she mentioned that Marty was in the hospital and was not doing very well. As soon as I read that post, it was like somebody took a shovel and hit me in the face with it. I knew right then exactly what Josh was trying to convey to his family. I just didn't know that Marty was as sick as he was. I had no idea. It all finally made sense. *Josh was telling me in the last four or so readings that Marty was about to pass and he was going to be there for him to make the transition easy. The soul that I so vividly described who was with Josh was actually Marty. Josh was trying to show that Marty was coming to join him.* Since I had not given Lisa the notes to the last four or five readings yet, I scribbled down a few notes on them, using an ink pen. I sealed them in an envelope and told Barb that when I got home from work the next day we had to go see Marty in the hospital. It was urgent and couldn't wait. Barb understood exactly what I was getting at after I explained the readings to her. She knew the importance and urgency in going to see Marty. The next evening, on the way to the hospital, I explained to Barb what I scribbled down on the notes from the readings. *I basically told Lisa, in the scribbling, that Josh was telling her in advance that Marty was coming to join him.* I told Barb there was no way that I could interfere with the life cycle process. I told her that I couldn't give Lisa that envelope. At least, not yet. I told Barb to give it to Lisa's mother, Janet. Don't ask me why I told Barb that, I just did. After arriving at the hospital we were greeted by Lisa and guess who? Yes, it was her mother, Janet. Janet was familiar with who I was. She had been reading my notes from all the previous readings with Marty and Lisa, and Barb was aware of this. While I was back in the intensive care unit visiting Marty with Lisa, Barb gave the envelope to Lisa's mother, Janet. She told her not to give it to Lisa yet. Barb told Janet to give her the envelope when she thought it was appropriate. She told her that we didn't want to interfere with the life cycle process. Barb told her that she was Lisa's mother and she would know when the appropriate time to do so would be. While I visited Marty, who was on life support, I held his hand and spoke to him telepathically. I told him that we loved him and his transition to the other side would be easy. It was very emotional. I cried briefly. Before exiting the hospital, Barb and I spoke briefly with Janet and Lisa. We both instantly liked Janet.

We liked the positive energy that she was spreading to Lisa. As Barb and I walked across the parking lot that evening to get into our truck, I told her that Marty was not doing very well at all. He was very, very sick. We walked to our truck not saying much, just kind of in shock from the entire situation. Whether we liked it or not, we were right in the middle of it. *I had to make sure that envelope was delivered before Marty passed. I wanted to make sure that Lisa would know in her heart for the rest of her life that her son, Josh, was telling her in advance what was going to happen, before it happened. I knew it was going to happen, I felt that strongly about it. The very next afternoon Marty passed to the other side.*

I took the day off from work to attend the funeral service for Marty. While Barb and I were looking at pictures displayed around the room, I took good notice to one in particular. *This was a picture of Marty as a teenager. In it he looked exactly like the soul that I was describing that Josh was showing me. I couldn't believe it. I pointed it out to Barb and without either of us saying a word, she smiled and knew exactly what I was talking about. Barb then mentioned that it was the only pictured displayed that had the front glass broken. It was cracked all the way across. I smiled and instantly knew that it was a validation from Josh to me. He knew that I got it and I got it right. It was an awesome sign from Josh on the other side!* Marty was a great husband and father. After hearing his nieces speak at the funeral, he must have been a great Uncle too. Marty left behind a loving, beautiful wife, Lisa, and two fine boys, Kyle and Dylan. Marty passed to the other side and joined Josh and his other relatives on February 17, 2016, he was only 51 years old. I figured that I did what Josh wanted and that was the end of it. It was time to move on, or at least that's what I thought.

In March and April of 2016, I did a few readings with Marty. I was trying to make that connection and see if I could get just a little information for Lisa, her mother, Janet, and other family members. In one of these readings I was shown a blue ribbon. I didn't know what it meant, but as usual I wrote it down in my notes. After reading my notes Lisa told me that someone from Marty's employer brought her home a box of awards that were in Marty's office at work. Also in that reading I mentioned that Marty showed me that Lisa kept something special in a drawer. I stated in the readings notes that I thought it might be a cross. Again after reading my notes, Lisa told me that she was going through things at the house and found an old small cross that Marty used to carry with him in his pocket when Josh was sick. She decided to keep it so she tucked it away in a drawer! Also in these readings, Marty was reaching out to his sons, Kyle and Dylan. He was sending his love and his protecting presence to both of them. I felt his emotion; he really loves those boys. Before Marty passed to the other side, he told Lisa that when he tried to contact her from the other side, he would call her "Baby Girl." After reading my notes, Lisa confirmed the following notes from my journal. In a reading in March I stated, *"I was shown a baby. Maybe Lisa called Marty a baby sometimes."* I didn't have it exactly right, but I did get the validating message for Lisa. *As with Wilma earlier in this book, Marty had fulfilled his death bed promise to contact Lisa from the other side!* This story of synchronicity just amazes me. Decades passed without Barb and me touching base with Lisa and Marty, yet their son, Josh, was able to reach out from the other side and bring this story full circle. The life paths of Lisa, Barb, and myself were put into motion years ago. Part of our journey has led us to where we are now. We took some terrible losses along the way, but we have learned so much from them. *I believe that Joshua wanted his story told!* He just used me as the messenger. I look forward to hearing from him in the future. In closing out this chapter I just have two words for Marty, Joshua, Lisa, Kyle, Dylan, Kelly, Janet, and their entire family, "PLAY BALL.'"

CHAPTER ELEVEN

The Healing

In this chapter I will briefly touch on some of my personal readings. There are some validations involved in the stories, but it is mostly about emotion and connecting. This book would not be complete without me adding some of my personal readings. After all, this book is about my journey with Spirit. It would not be an honest, complete account, if I did not add some of my most intimate readings and stories. I figure if I can tell how I held my son as he took his last breaths, like I did earlier in this book, then I can finish telling the complete story. It would not be complete and honest if I did not include this chapter.

It was February of 2015, and I had just learned how to initiate contact with the other side. Obviously, I wanted desperately to have contact with Cathy, David, my dad, and other relatives. Making these connections was very high on my priority list. In this particular reading on February 15th, I was able to make contact with my son, David. Before I connected with David in this reading, this was my experience. I found myself walking up a hill. When I got to the top of the hill, I noticed that it overlooked a city of lights. It seemed to have a religious meaning. I saw a church bell and steeple. I went down to the city's edge, but didn't go in. It was very peaceful. I had to mention this part of the reading because it was in my notes. I had forgotten about these notes and stumbled upon them when doing my research. This story definitely goes hand in hand with my story earlier in this book about Jesus and the *City of Light*. Wow, just another piece of synchronicity! In this reading, David let me know that when he was in the hospital on that dreadful night, he wanted to stay with me, and be with me, though he knew that he couldn't. He showed me an image. It was a two-second film clip, but I will never forget it as long as I live. It was an image of a medium blue light at the ceiling level of his hospital room. From his body came a second medium blue orb of light, just like the one at ceiling level. They were both about the size of a cantaloupe. The one that came out of David's body met up with the one at ceiling level. They joined together and instantly went through the ceiling and disappeared. David let me know that this was his soul joining his mother's soul and that they left together. I felt his emotion. He was in a happy place, and on top of that, he was with his mother. David also let me know that there were two angels there that night, beside me, bedside. I always felt that there was a presence there that night. I just didn't understand it until now. This personal reading alone was reason enough for me to celebrate God, be happy, heal, and move forward with my life. I can't tell you enough how much this little short story has healed me. I felt his emotion in this reading, I will never forget it as long as I live. This story also is enough in itself to make me want to connect other people with loved ones on the other side. I know firsthand how much healing can be done from a single reading.

In March of 2015, I connected with Cathy. In this reading she showed me the number 82. I wrote it down in my notes not knowing what it meant. At the time, it didn't ring a bell. Next, she started putting images into my mind, such as things that we did and places that we went when we first got together. Things only she and I would understand. Then it dawned on me, everything she was showing me happened in 1982. Thus, the number 82. I instantly recognized and knew that she was very vividly validating her presence there with me. I knew right then that I had again met up with my first wife, Cathy.

When I put forth the thought of David to her, she smiled from ear to ear. It was a monumental day in my life.

In a reading that I did in April of 2015, I connected with David, but Cathy stepped forward. What she let me know in this reading was tremendous. Cathy let me know that on the night of the accident, she died instantly, and did not suffer. She let me know that her spirit, or soul, came out of her body right away. She said that she stayed with David the entire time to comfort him. Remember, David died 24 hours after Cathy. She stayed with David from the time of the accident all the way through the time at the hospital where he took his last breaths as he lay in my arms; she never left him. Cathy let me know that she was there soothing and calming David as he lay dying. This reading was the perfect fit. Cathy was a great mother. Cathy and David were always together; she never left his side. You have no idea how good this made me feel. This reading really warmed my heart. It also confirmed my reading with David about that same dreadful night. I always knew that I sensed a presence in the hospital room that night, but didn't understand what it meant. Now I understood; Cathy was among angels in the room, waiting to take our son to the other side. *I do think that things happen for a reason. I think on this dreadful November night in 1986, the powers from the other side allowed me to hold, kiss, say goodbye, and tell my son that I loved him one last time. He had started his new journey with his mother, my wife, Cathy.*

It was May of 2015. I did a reading and connected with my dad. This reading just flat out blew me away. At first, I couldn't figure out what was going on, but everything made sense as I got further into the reading. In this reading, Dad took me by the hand and led me to the edge of the white light. I was a little boy. I couldn't figure it out at first. I kept thinking, "Who is this little boy?" and "Why is Dad holding my hand?" The edge of the bright light felt so familiar. Next he let me know that when I was a little boy and had my eye surgery, I had been to this area. He let me know that it wasn't my time to go then, but I was on the edge. I always knew it felt like I had someone watching over me my entire life; this was why. My guardian angels were with me at that point in my life and had been with me ever since. Upon entering the edge of the bright light area in this reading I felt their presence and recognized the feeling I have had my entire life. It was the same feeling. This really hit home because the only thing that I remembered from my eye surgery as a five year old child was the operating room light. It wasn't until the night of this reading, 46 years later that I realized and found out what that light that I remembered really was. It all finally made sense to me. ***My whole life made more sense to me at this very moment!***

Also in the summer of 2015, I had several readings with my dad. Most of them involved him showing me images and filling my mind with information. He always showed me my siblings as they were when they were younger. Of course my siblings and our mom are still with us today, but I believe he was just trying to show me things as they were when he was in the prime of his life before he got sick. He also showed me my mother in the same time frame when the three of us kids were little. Obviously, he was showing me things that were important to him, the time that he spent with us, and how he was there for us. We have always missed Dad, but it is so nice to be able to touch base with him occasionally.

As I have briefly touched upon earlier in this book, I have on occasion tried doing a reading using an EMF device. These devices pick up on energy fields. They use these devices on television shows that deal with the paranormal. When this particular device of mine picks up on an energy source, it beeps three times and has a small red light that illuminates. On the rare occasion that I do a session like this, I also use an EVP device. This is just a digital voice recorder. I have only done these kind of sessions a handful of times. I have had very good success using these devices, but I just don't do them very often; it is mainly a time issue. Remember, I work full time and then some. I just don't have time to do everything that I want to do and do it all the time. It seems that I am most successful with these devices in the middle of the night. The experts say that in the middle of the night most people are sleeping so there is less negative energy in play. That makes it easier for Spirit to get through to us. I definitely would have to agree with that statement, just from my experiences alone. The way that I do a session using these devices is as follows: I do a normal reading, except I am in a living room chair because Barb is sleeping in our room. I don't want to risk any contamination to the session. I have on my ear muffs as usual to block out noise. I have my pad of paper on the left arm of the living room chair. I set the digital recorder on the coffee table to the left of my chair. I put the EMF device on the right arm of the chair. I do the reading as I usually do, with my eyes closed, around 4 am in the morning. When I start getting information, I reach for my pad of paper and take notes.

On the night of November 1st, 2015, I was doing a session in the aforementioned manner. I was connecting with my dad. When I started getting information in the reading, I grabbed my note pad and jotted down the information. It went as any reading went and was normal. Out of curiosity I played back the recording from the digital recorder from my session. *I was listening and hoping to hear my dad's voice. I kept hoping and listening, but no, there was nothing to be heard. What happened next just completely blew me out of the water.* I was not expecting it at all. As I was listening, I heard the EMF device make three beeps. Within 10 seconds of the three beeps from the device, I could hear me pick up my pad of paper and start writing my notes. The rustling noise that the papers in the notebook made as I opened up the pages, came through loud and clear. *I could not believe what I heard. First, the EMF device picked up an energy source, then I picked up my note pad signifying that I also had picked up on Spirit. I had my first electronic proof of my connecting to Spirit!* What made the session even more remarkable was the fact that during the reading I didn't know that the EMF device went off. The reason was because I had on my ear muffs. Secondly, I didn't see the small red light on the EMF device illuminate either. The reason was because I am blind in my right eye. Even in a dark room when a small light illuminates I can't tell that it's there because my right eye is completely dead. My eyes were closed, but it didn't matter. I had accidentally set up the session to work out perfectly and didn't even realize it until after the fact. ***I had electronic proof that I had connected to my dad. I was overwhelmed!*** I want to mention that I have also had similar successes using this method with Wilma, and also with Barb's dad. As good as these sessions were, I just haven't used the method very often. That may change in the future.

In the fall of 2015, I had a reading where our previous family pet "Lassie" connected with me. Lassie was a Collie just like the original Lassie on television. She was our family pet for 15 years. When I was outside, at home, she was my shadow. If I was working on a car in the garage, she would lay on the floor and watch me. If I went outside, she would follow me. She literally was my best friend. I still miss her today. In this particular reading, I saw Lassie as a young adult dog. She was in her prime and was well manicured. She looked good. She was also laying on her side and kind of gnawing at me with her mouth, like she used to do. The next day I told Barb and my daughter, Jennifer, about the reading. Jennifer stated that she had dreamt about Lassie that very night. She also saw her exactly as I did, in her prime and gnawing with her mouth. Jennifer said that I was freaking her out. Thank you Lassie for letting us know that you are still roaming around here on your old stomping grounds!

In a reading in January of 2016, I connected with my dad. At the time, one of my siblings was looking at houses in another state. In this reading Dad showed me a house that this sibling would move into. It had a very odd front entryway and porch. Later, this sibling sent me a picture of the house that they were going to move into. At the time, my sibling knew nothing about the reading. The picture sent to me of the house had a very weird looking entryway and front porch. I will admit it was not exactly as I had seen it, but it validated that Dad was at that house while on their journey to another state.

This story is short but shows that Spirit is always with us, whether we know it or not. Thanks, Dad!

I would like to also mention that in some readings I have connected with Cathy's dad. He was my father-in-law. He is a kind spirit. I mention this for Cathy's family. Good people.

In closing out this chapter, I would like to again say thank you to Wilma. If it weren't for her persistency, I would have never written this book. I also never would have healed from my losses. These personal readings healed me. I say again, ***these personal readings healed me!***

Top: My dad in 1961, as a 19 year old.

Bottom: Dad with my son, David Ray, 1983. Photo taken right before
Dad took sick. Also about 3 years before David lost his life here on earth.

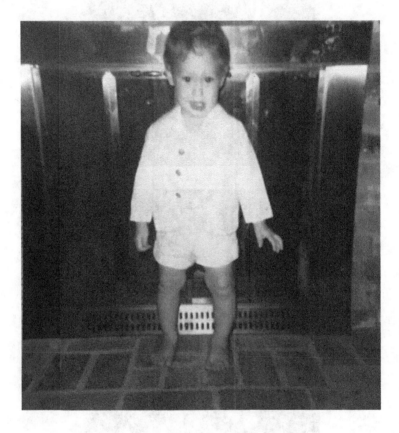

This is a picture of David Ray Jacobs.

CHAPTER TWELVE

Summarizing

Now, even after 18 months of doing readings, I still sometimes wonder if it is real. Even with all of the validations that I have, it does still sometimes seem unreal. I do understand though, that it is real, and I love making those connections. I sometimes feel like a magician trying to pull a bunny out of a hat for a crowd. When I connect to Spirit for a sitter, they have to understand that it is not a question and answer session. Most of what I get is what they show or tell me, it is not a normal conversation. It involves symbols, emotion, images, and phrases. There is almost like a new language that you have to learn when doing readings. You have to learn how to decipher the symbols and signs. Laura Lynne Jackson says it very well in her book "The Light Between Us." She notes that it is like learning a new alphabet or language. She is absolutely correct. It took me about a year of doing readings to figure that out, but it is very important. The best advice I can give anyone wanting to learn to connect to the other side is, don't try to make it happen, let it happen. The harder you try, the less results you likely will get. Now as far as percentages go for me in a reading, it can vary. In some readings I can just feel it. I know when I get a good connection. In these readings I probably have a 75% or better hit rate in accuracy. In some readings I might have a 50% accuracy rate, but a lot of times I think maybe the sitter doesn't realize some things are a hit until after the fact. There are occasions when I do have readings that I just don't connect very well and I get a misread, but not very often. I can usually get some kind of information from Spirit. They are usually there, you just have to tune in to the right frequency to connect to them. Also, I might add here, that throughout this book when I had validation stories and stories about connecting to the other side, I didn't mention much about how a sitter's relatives send their love. They do send their love a lot and I pass that message on all the time, but throughout this book I was wanting to show validating evidence. Any Medium can say, "Aunt Susie loves you." It may be true, and probably is, but that doesn't prove to the sitter that you are connected to their loved one. I try to get at least one piece of very good validating information in every reading. I try to be an evidential medium. I always only tell what I see and am told whether it means anything to the sitter or not. The most important thing that I can tell you about the afterlife is that it is all about love. Let me repeat that, *it is all about love*. Like I have mentioned before, I don't go to heaven when I do readings. *I have only been in the presence of God on one occasion.* Most of the time when I do a reading I am in a place of consciousness only. There are times that I am in a very beautiful place, or in a certain setting. Even in a particular environment in a reading, but usually I am just in a different place of consciousness.

I have mentioned that I have meditated throughout my life; I highly recommend it to anyone. There are only three places on earth that I have been where I have heard complete silence, and I do mean complete silence. Not in the woods hunting, where you still hear noises even on a very quiet day. Not on a still, calm lake, in the morning. I have only heard complete silence and peace on a sailboat on the ocean at daybreak, out past where the waves break. I have heard this peace and silence at the top of a mountain in the Rocky Mountain National Park. The only other place on earth that I have experienced this complete silence and peace is in deep meditation; it is very therapeutic. It is a very nice and healing place for the soul to be. Once you get some practice and get decent at holding your meditation for longer periods of 30 minutes to an hour, you can really help yourself. Not only mentally, but I believe, physically, too. Take me for an example. I have meditated throughout my life and I go to the doctor about every 10 years. Not to say that won't change as I start to age, but I think that meditation has played a part in my health. *Even if you are not interested in connecting to the other side, I highly recommend meditation to anyone. I really believe it is a very healthy addition to anyone's lifestyle. Remember, meditation can be in prayer, and also praying.*

Now there are people out there that know me and probably think that I have been a hard person in my life, that I was just worried about myself and not anybody else. To tell you the truth, there were times when they were probably right, to a degree. It wasn't that I didn't care about other people. I am a very emotional person. I just never was one to show it publicly. With the life that I had as a young man, and young adult, it can make you hard. Not selfish, just hard. Like I mentioned earlier when you have major tragedies in your life and you have no one to fall back on at a young age, you kind of have to become a little hard in your life. You know that if something goes wrong you have to deal with it. You can't go to mommy and daddy to solve your problems, the buck stops here. It is on your plate, and you know it. When you are 20 years old, on your own with no safety net, as I was, you have to put yourself and family first because you know if you don't, nobody else is going to. I always put my wife and kids first in my life. Everyone and everything else was second. I hear some middle aged people complain about their parents sometimes and I think, they don't know how lucky they are to have someone to go to with their problems. Always understand that the young people out there with no family, parents, or siblings, have a different life than most people. They have to cut their own path in life. It does make life more difficult. With all the tragedy I had in my life as a young man, I have never been bitter. I will admit that at times I may have felt cheated, but never bitter. *Also keep in mind that those young people out there that have had tragic events happen to them, the damage is done. Whether it be parent loss, abuse, being orphaned, being handicapped, deaths, or whatever. The damage is done. There is no taking that back in their life. Their life path will always be different from most people.* I know that I am going off subject a little bit here, but these were points that affected me in my life and were worth mentioning. I have been there and done that. This information will help people that read this book understand my life circumstances better.

As I have mentioned, I have gone to church quite a bit throughout my life. I have also read the Bible completely. I also read over half of it a second time, but for some reason I stopped halfway through. I kind of felt like Forrest Gump when he was jogging across the country and just decided to stop and go home. The only thing that really doesn't add up to me in the Bible is in the Old Testament. In the Old Testament, as I recall, God is described as a "Jealous God." He literally kills hundreds of thousands of people with a vengeance. *This is not the God that I was in the presence of. The God that I was in the presence of was all about love and understanding. He was about nothing else. I felt it. I knew it. God doesn't care what color you are and God doesn't care if you are gay or straight. God is only Love and Light.* So yes, I do believe in God, I have been in his presence, but that is a point that I have to make or I wouldn't be honest. I don't understand it, but I just explain things as I see them. I also think that most people do go to heaven and the afterlife. Some people may be further down the pipeline than others, meaning that they probably aren't in God's light as much as other souls are. ***IT IS FROM MY EXPERIENCE THAT IF ONLY PERFECT PEOPLE WENT TO HEAVEN, THEN HEAVEN WOULD BE A VERY LONELY PLACE!***

I have mentioned in a couple of spots (no pun intended) throughout this book that I have connected with pets on the other side. Yes, they are there and do have souls. They are a part of the spirit world. I have also had pets come up in readings that were still here on the earth plane, being used as a validation point. But, yes, it is from my experiences that pets are in heaven and the afterlife.

There are a lot of people out there that have known me for 20 years and don't even know about my first wife Cathy, and son, David. It is not that I kept them a secret my entire life, it just hurt too badly to talk about them. Though, not since connecting to them in the afterlife. That is a very healing thing to do, making those connections. *I have healed so much from afterlife connections that it has changed my life.* I can now, for the first time in my life, talk about Cathy and David and be all right with it. I know where they are, what it feels like, and I love it. Also, and very importantly, I didn't want to have a crutch for the rest of my life. I didn't want to be known as the guy who lost his wife and son. I didn't use my eye as a crutch when I was a child and I didn't want my life tragedies to be a crutch either. I faced life head on. It wasn't easy at times but that is how I did it. Now that I am older and my kids are raised, I can slow down in life. I can relax a little bit more, and talk about things easier. I just try to go with the flow.

As I finish summarizing this book I would like to say that I have always put my wife and kids first. My family came first in my life, and I have never regretted this decision. After losing Cathy and David at an early age, I found out what was important in life. No, don't get me wrong I'm not perfect by any means. I've made a ton of mistakes and still do, but that is how you learn. You have to move forward. To tell you the truth, I can't remember the last time that I really got mad about anything. Working with Spirit on a regular basis and meditating take a lot of negative thoughts out of your mind. Connecting with Spirit has changed my life. Now don't get me wrong, like I said, I'm not perfect. I can be driving down the interstate and when somebody cuts me off, I will cuss them, then laugh about it to myself and with Spirit. I also try to avoid what Garth Brooks would call "Low Places", because if somebody asks me to dance enough times I'm probably going to jail. Throughout all the setbacks and hard times in my life, I never wanted to be anybody else. There were times when I wished things could have been different, but I was always comfortable with who I was. I never wanted to be anybody else.

Now I want to touch on hard work. These experiences that I've had didn't come easy a lot of times. I have worked very hard at being a medium. You have to put in a lot of time. Yes, I think a lot of mediumship skills can come naturally for some people, but even those people have to work hard at what they do. I have studied very hard. I have meditated and connected to the other side many times, every week. I have, and still am working very hard to improve and maintain my mediumship skills. I have learned so much from Spirit. They have taught me so much, but I believe that it is only the tip of the iceberg. There is so much more for me to learn. I am so anxious and excited to move forward and keep learning and helping other people. My life has so much more purpose now. The main reason that I wrote this book was so that my family would know the real me. *Like I said early in this book, the truth of my life is written in these pages.* And I have to tell you, it is so liberating, and feels so good not to have my life events buried inside me anymore. *I was planning on taking what I knew with me to my grave. But God, Wilma, and Wilma's girls stepped into my life's path and altered my future in such a terrific way. Joshua and his family have also had a dramatic impact on my life and healing.* Yes, I do believe things happen for a reason and I do believe in synchronicity. Just take my life with Barb as one example. *Remember, I heard a voice at Cathy and David's funeral tell me that I was going to marry Barb next. I didn't even really know her at the time. But decades later, look at where we are and how Spirit and God have brought us even closer. If I am never able to connect again, I have told my story and it is the absolute truth with no exaggerations. I am very content with where I am at in my life, but hope to learn so much more.*

In the future I want to be able to read anyone, anywhere, at any time. That is my goal and what I am starting to work on now. There is so much to learn. *I have decided that the only thing I'm going to take with me to my grave is the comfort of having helped people heal and having told my story!*

This is a picture of me and my beautiful wife, Barb.

Final Thoughts

I spent a lot of my younger years not wanting to be different. I have found out that I love being different! See you on the other side!

Acknowledgements

I want to thank God for giving me that one brief moment of time to be in his light and love. God's light, and my connections to the other side have HEALED ME!

Acknowledgments

Appendix A

The following is a list of some of the books that I have read in the last 18 months. They are in no particular order. The author is the heading, followed by the names of the books.

Suzanne Giesemann
Messages of Hope, The Priest and the Medium, Wolf's Message, In the Silence, Love beyond Words

Janet Nohavec and Suzanne Giesemann
Where Two Worlds Meet, Through the Darkness

James Van Praagh
Talking to Heaven, Ghosts Among Us, Adventures of the Soul, Heaven and Earth, When Heaven Touches Earth, Growing Up in Heaven, The Power of Love, Unfinished Business

R. Craig Hogan PH.D.
Afterlife Communication, New Developments in Afterlife Communication, Aspects of Consciousness

John Burke
Imagine Heaven

Theresa Caputo
You Can't Make This Stuff Up, There's more to Life than This

George Anderson
Lessons from the Light, Conversations with the Other Side

Blair Robertson
Afterlife Connections, Psychic Development, Spirit
Guides, Afterlife 3 Easy Ways to Connect and
Communicate With Your Deceased Loved Ones

Pete A Sanders JR.
You Are Psychic

Victor & Wendy Zammit
A Lawyer Presents the Evidence for the Afterlife

Laura Lynne Jackson
The Light between Us

Stewart Alexander
An Extraordinary Journey. The Memoirs of a Physical Medium

Alastair I.M. Rae
Quantum Physics

Sanaya Roman

Duane Packer
Opening to Channel How to Connect With Your Guide

Sanaya Roman
Soul Love

Kevin Todeschi
Edgar Cayce on Vibrations Spirit in Motion,
Edgar Cayce on the Akashic Records

Kevin Todeschi

Carol Ann Liaros
Auras & Colors

William A. McGarey, MD
Edgar Cayce on Healing Foods

Thomas Sugrue
The Story of Edgar Cayce There Is a River

Appendix B

If you are interested in connecting to the other side, or even just expanding your knowledge, I would suggest studying the following subjects. A lot of this information is in the books in Appendix A. I'm sure the information is also in a lot of other books as well. These subjects seem to tie in together, and be a part of the greater whole. Remember, always keep an open mind and stay in the white light of God.

1. Meditation
2. Colors and Auras
3. Numerology
4. Tarot Cards
5. Electronic Devices
6. Books
7. Online Courses
8. Classroom Courses
9. Chakras
10. A lot of hard work

Bibliography

Barry, Jeff. Greenwich, Ellie. Spector, Phil. (1964). *Chapel of Love.* (Recorded by The Dixie Cups). On *Chapel of Love.* [Vinyl]. USA. Red Bird Records.

Blackwell, Dewayne. Lee, Earl Bud. (1989). *Friends in Low Places.* (Recorded by Garth Brooks). On No Fences Album. [CD or Vinyl]. USA. Capitol Nashville.

Burke, John. *Imagine Heaven.* Michigan. Baker Books. 2015.

Capra, Frank. (Producer and Director). (1946). *It's a Wonderful Life.* USA. Liberty Films.

Giesemann, Suzanne. *Messages of Hope.* USA. One Mind Books. 2011.

Giesemann, Suzanne. *The Priest and the Medium.* USA. Hay House. 2009.

Hogan, Dr. R. Craig (Editor). *Afterlife Communication, 16 Proven Methods, 85 True Accounts.* Florida. Academy for Spiritual and Consciousness Studies. 2014.

Jackson, Laura Lynne. *The Light Between Us.* New York. Spiegel and Grau. 2015.

Jaffe, Steven-Charles. Weinstein, Lisa. Koch, Howard (Producers). Zucker, Jerry (Director). (1990). *Ghost*. USA. Paramount Pictures.

Johnson, Mark (Producer). Levinson, Barry (Director). (1988). *Rain Man*. USA. United Artists.

McBroom, Amanda. (1979). *The Rose*. (Recorded by Bette Midler). On *The Rose*. Atlantic.

Nohavec, Janet. Giesemann, Suzanne. *Where Two Worlds Meet, How to Develop Evidential Mediumship*. California. Aventine Press. 2010.

Roman, Sanaya. Packer, Duane. *Opening to Channel, How to Connect to your Guide*. California. H.J. Kramer INC. 1989.

Schwartz, Sherwood (Producer). (1964). *Gilligan's Island* (Television Series). USA. United Artists.

Tisch, Steve. Starkey, Steve. Finerman, Wendy (Producers). Zemeckis, Robert (Director). (1994). *Forrest Gump*. USA. Paramount Pictures.

Todeschi, Kevin J. *Dream Images and Symbols*. USA. A.R.E. Press. 1995.

Wrather, Jack. Golden, Robert. Granville, Bonita. Maxwell, Robert. Rudolph, Abel. Beaudine Jr., William. Bruce, Dusty. Harris, Sherman. Castle, Don. Frank, Peter. Fromkess, Leon. (Producers). (1954). *Lassie* (Television Series). California. The series starting in 1954 was a CBS production.